Dynamic READ-ALOUD STRATEGIES
for English Learners

Building Language and Literacy in the Primary Grades

Peggy Hickman and Sharolyn D. Pollard-Durodola

INTERNATIONAL Reading Association
800 BARKSDALE ROAD, PO BOX 8139
NEWARK, DE 19714-8139, USA
www.reading.org

The International Reading Association attempts, through its publications, to provide a forum for a wide spectrum of opinions on reading. This policy permits divergent viewpoints without implying the endorsement of the Association.

Executive Editor, Books   Corinne M. Mooney
Developmental Editor   Charlene M. Nichols
Developmental Editor   Tori Mello Bachman
Developmental Editor   Stacey L. Reid
Editorial Production Manager   Shannon T. Fortner
Design and Composition Manager   Anette Schuetz

Project Editors   Stacey L. Reid and Rebecca A. Fetterolf

Cover   Design, Lise Holliker Dykes; Photograph, © 2008 Jupiterimages Corporation

Library of Congress Cataloging-in-Publication Data

Hickman, Peggy, 1967-
  Dynamic read-aloud strategies for English learners : building language and literacy in the primary grades / Peggy Hickman and Sharolyn D. Pollard-Durodola.
       p. cm.
  Includes bibliographical references and index.
  ISBN 978-0-87207-596-2
  1. Oral reading--United States. 2. English language--Study and teaching (Primary)--United States--Foreign speakers. 3. Second language acquisition--United States. I. Pollard-Durodola, Sharolyn D., 1959- II. Title.
  LB1573.5.H53 2009
  372.45'2--dc22

                                                                2008046487

To all teachers who make a difference in their students' lives every day.
—Peggy Hickman

To Haile and Jonothon Durodola, who love books.
—Sharolyn D. Pollard-Durodola

CONTENTS

Peggy Hickman is an assistant professor of education at Arcadia University in Glenside, Pennsylvania, USA. She is passionate about helping teachers and school administrators in diverse cultural and linguistic environments understand the needs of English-language learners in general and special education programs. She teaches undergraduate, master's level, and doctoral level courses in multicultural special education; multilingual and multicultural assessment; language, diversity, and schooling; and emergent literacy and biliteracy. In addition to these topics, Hickman conducts extensive professional development with teachers and districts to respond to the needs of diverse student populations. She has also presented on these topics regionally, nationally, and, most recently, at the International Reading Association World Congress in Costa Rica.

Hickman's undergraduate studies were in early childhood education at the University of Vermont, Burlington. She has two master's degrees: an MEd in elementary/bilingual education from Arizona State University and a second MEd in educational administration from the University of Texas at Austin. While in Texas she coordinated local and national research projects on emergent reading in English and Spanish. She has published articles in *Learning Disabilities Quarterly*, *Exceptional Children*, and *The Reading Teacher*, and she is currently completing a second book for school administrators related to educating culturally and linguistically diverse students with and without disabilities in school settings.

Peggy's passion for these topics originated during her nine-year teaching career, when she taught bilingual Spanish–English students in prekindergarten through second-grade classrooms in Arizona and Texas. She has taught in multiage, multigrade, and dual language settings, as well as single-grade bilingual classrooms with majority Spanish speakers (she is fluent and literate in Spanish). Her desire to reach all of her students led her to pursue her doctorate in multicultural special education at the University of Texas, Austin.

Sharolyn Pollard-Durodola is an assistant professor of bilingual programs at Texas A&M University in College Station, USA. Her research interests are in the area of early literacy in Spanish and English, with an emphasis on vocabulary acquisition and early reading interventions. She specifically focuses on developing intervention curricula that build on empirically validated instructional design principles and evaluating their impact on the language and reading development of second-language learners by attending to both oral language (vocabulary) and comprehension needs.

Pollard-Durodola's undergraduate studies were in Romance languages with an emphasis on Spanish and Portuguese at Mount Holyoke College in South Hadley, Massachusetts, USA. She has two master's degrees: an MAT in teaching Spanish from Teachers College, Columbia University in New York City and an MS in developmental reading from City University of New York, New York City. Her doctorate is in curriculum and instruction with an emphasis on second-language acquisition and bilingual education. She has presented at national conferences on early Spanish literacy and vocabulary interventions for second-language learners and at-risk populations.

She is a coprincipal investigator on a project funded by the U.S. Department of Education Institute of Education Sciences that investigates the acceleration of vocabulary and listening comprehension skills in English- and Spanish-speaking preschool children through a shared-book reading intervention. Her scholarship and publications are focused on a range of learners from preschool to fourth grade. She worked for 14 years as a public school teacher and school administrator.

Author Information for Correspondence
Peggy and Sharolyn welcome questions and feedback from readers.
Peggy can be reached at hickmanp@arcadia.edu.
Sharolyn can be reached at sdurodola@tamu.edu.

PREFACE

The goal of *Dynamic Read-Aloud Strategies for English Learners: Building Language and Literacy in the Primary Grades* is to demonstrate to teachers how a read-aloud activity that most of them already use in the classroom every day can be used as a strategy to help second-language learners develop listening comprehension and oral language proficiency in a culturally and linguistically appropriate way (Morrow & Brittain, 2003). We believe such a goal is extremely relevant, given the fact that more and more of America's teachers face the challenge of meeting the needs of English-language learners (ELLs)—students from diverse cultural and linguistic backgrounds who are acquiring English as a second language (ESL).

Consider the demographics. In 2000, according to the Federal Interagency Forum on Child and Family Statistics (2002), about 11% of the U.S. population, or 32 million people, were foreign born. Furthermore, approximately one in five children were from immigrant families. Currently, approximately 5% of all school-age children speak a language other than English at home.

The implications for classroom teachers are significant. During the 2002–2003 academic year, 5 million ELLs enrolled in U.S. elementary and secondary schools, an increase of 84% from 1992 (National Clearinghouse for English Language Acquisition, 2004). And according to the latest figures available, almost 10% of the national public school population is made up of ELLs (National Clearinghouse for English Language Acquisition, 2004).

These students bring with them a wealth of diverse characteristics. For example, some are recent immigrants, while others represent the second or third generation of their families born in the United States. Some have had prior formal schooling experiences; others have not. Some are refugees, fleeing war and significant loss in their home country. Some face high mobility rates within urban or rural communities. As a whole, they speak more than 400 languages, although 75–80% are native Spanish speakers (Kindler, 2002).

Such a scenario demands that an ever-growing number of teachers become proficient at educating students from diverse cultural and linguistic backgrounds. Key to that mastery is knowledge and application of current research in the area of language and literacy development as it pertains to ELLs. In fact, we believe the future welfare of such children depends upon teachers' ability to translate compelling and promising research findings in this area into effective instructional practices.

The procedure we describe in this book was a critical piece of an experimental intervention study we conducted that was designed to look at how teachers build the literacy, oral language, and listening comprehension skills of first-grade Spanish-speaking ELLs in monolingual and bilingual literacy settings (Hickman, Pollard-Durodola, & Vaughn, 2004). The students who participated in the study were from seven elementary schools located in geographical areas with a high density of ELLs: two urban school districts in Texas and one district located along the Texas–Mexico border. Four of the schools in the study were rated as *exemplary* and three as *recognized* based on student performance on state accountability measures. As a result, we concluded that the schools were successful in providing literacy instruction to most students on campus and were teaching students to read in environments conducive to learning (Vaughn, Linan-Thompson, & Hickman, 2003).

As part of our study, students participated in strategic read-aloud lessons that were based on a scope and sequence that explicitly and systematically developed oral vocabulary, listening comprehension, and general oral language skills in Spanish or English (Vaughn, Cirino et al., 2006; Vaughn et al., 2005; Vaughn, Mathes et al., 2006). The lessons were designed to reflect a number of key research findings on effective language and literacy development for ELLs, including the importance of (a) connecting and building upon students' cultural and linguistic experiences as they relate to textual material; (b) scaffolding students' second-language instruction; and (c) providing students with opportunities to develop language skills, including vocabulary development and listening comprehension, through small-group, structured literacy activities.

The students who took part in the study received 50 minutes of daily reading instruction in small groups from a trained bilingual teacher in English or Spanish, depending on the language of the students' core reading instruction. During the first 40 minutes of instruction, students took part in 6–10 short activities that addressed simple to complex skills across a variety of instructional strands, including phonemic awareness, letter knowledge, word study, listening comprehension, and fluency building. The last 10 minutes of instruction was spent on the strategic read-aloud procedure (again, in Spanish or English, depending on the language of instruction) described in detail in this text.

We found that, after seven months, the students who received daily, intensive reading instruction in English outperformed students in the contrast group in the areas of phonological awareness, letter–sound knowledge, word attack, spelling dictation, and passage comprehension (Vaughn, Cirino et al., 2006; Vaughn, Mathes et al., 2006). Students who received instruction in Spanish also made impressive literacy gains, outperforming students in the contrast group in the areas of phonemic awareness, word attack, word reading, reading comprehension, fluency, and language development in Spanish (Vaughn et al., 2005). For more detail on the intervention studies and our findings, please see the Appendix.

We believe both new and experienced teachers as well as content specialists can successfully use this procedure to strategically build the academic language of primary-grade (K–2) ELLs. What's more, the procedures can be used across a variety of educational settings, including general education classrooms where teachers provide literacy instruction to ELLs in English; general education, bilingual classrooms where teachers provide literacy instruction to ELLs in Spanish; resource, pull-out, or inclusive ESL programs; and reading resource rooms.

Teachers who have experience teaching ELLs or bilingual students will find the book helpful in specifying the ways in which the core elements of this procedure align with research-based principles of effective instruction for those learning a second language. Moreover, strategies described in this text have been shown to be particularly helpful for ELLs who are below the level of their peers in literacy acquisition (Vaughn et al., 2005; Vaughn, Linan-Thompson et al., 2006). As a result, teachers can use the practices we describe to provide intensive, explicit early language experiences for students who may need additional support in reaching language and literacy benchmarks. Yet, by scaffolding instruction in ways we discuss, teachers can also differentiate instruction for learners who are meeting grade-level targets.

Likewise, teachers working in bilingual or monolingual English instructional settings who are new to teaching ELLs will find the information in this book helpful, not only in terms of the specifics it offers relative to implementing the read-aloud procedure but also because of the general framework it provides for supporting the overall language and literacy skill acquisition of ELLs.

Because Spanish speakers make up almost 80% of all ELLs (Kindler, 2002) in the United States and bilingual programs in many states focus on first-language literacy for this population, we have provided some examples of text and vocabulary used in strategic read-aloud lessons in Spanish. Teachers are urged to adapt their lessons as necessary for non–Spanish-speaking students who are acquiring literacy in their home language as a core academic skill by attending to the principles we discuss.

Chapter 1 summarizes the research behind the strategic read-aloud procedure described in this book and presents a visual representation and brief overview of the 10 steps involved in designing and carrying it out. Detailed descriptions of each step are presented in the following chapters. Chapter 2 provides a guide for grouping students for strategic read-aloud lessons and selecting appropriate texts to use during those lessons. It also describes how teachers can use the read-aloud experience to effectively activate and build content knowledge. Chapter 3 explores the relationship between the strategic selection and teaching of vocabulary and the development of a student's oral language proficiency, and it also describes ways to actively engage students in the process of learning new words and generalizing them across settings. Chapter 4 guides teachers in scaffolding their instruction to effectively build listening comprehension before, during, and after read-aloud lessons. And Chapter 5 shows how all the steps in the process are woven together in daily, sequential lessons that strategically support vocabulary development and listening comprehension.

Each chapter includes examples of pertinent strategies and procedures that have proven successful in supporting students' vocabulary and comprehension skills. All teacher and student names used in this book are pseudonyms, and all classroom dialogue, diaries, and quoted material are composite sketches that represent real teachers, students, and classroom situations that we have encountered in our studies. Also included in each chapter is a Research to Practice section that prompts readers to reflect on ideas presented in the chapter and includes a list of suggested readings for those who wish to further their knowledge in each area.

Again, the goal of *Dynamic Read-Aloud Strategies for English Learners: Building Language and Literacy in the Primary Grades* is twofold: (1) to provide teachers with the theoretical knowledge they need to understand the process of second-language development and (2) to describe in detail a proven strategy that will help them effectively apply that knowledge to their work with ELLs.

CHAPTER 1

Strategic Read-Aloud Lessons: What the Research Says

Mrs. Lee:	*(first-grade, general education classroom teacher) During story retelling, Manuel does not participate as much as [the other students]…because he is repeating what the other kids are saying. He tries hard. I briefly explain to him what is going on in the story and I tell him to pay close attention to the pictures. This helps him understand better… The other kids are able to remember what happened in the story and always want to participate. (Journal Entry, November 2002)*
Ms. Octavio:	*(second-grade, bilingual education classroom teacher) Linda sigue teniendo dificultad para expresarse, no le salen las palabras, se paraliza. Me dice la maestra que ella tampoco ha podido sacarle palabras. (Diario, marzo 2003)*
Translation:	*Linda continues having difficulty expressing herself; the words won't come out, she becomes paralyzed. Her teacher tells me that neither has she been able to pull the words out [get her to express herself]. (Journal Entry, March 2003)*

Mrs. Lee, a monolingual, English-speaking teacher in a large urban school, is concerned that some of her first-grade ELLs do not participate in class discussions about the books she reads aloud to the class. Ms. Octavio, an experienced bilingual teacher and native Spanish speaker, worries about the difficulty her students have understanding challenging academic vocabulary and unfamiliar content that has little to do with their own lives. Such problems make discussions about texts difficult.

Although the dilemmas faced by these teachers are familiar to most educators, they are also confounding and raise perplexing pedagogical questions:

- How can teachers help second-language learners from diverse cultural and linguistic backgrounds to comprehend and respond to challenging texts that include content significantly different from their own experiences?

- How can teachers of ELLs effectively scaffold instruction for students who are still in the process of acquiring oral language proficiency?

• How can teachers influence the development of oral literacy and listening comprehension skills in students who have difficulty reading and comprehending in their primary or secondary language and do so in ways that are culturally and linguistically appropriate and responsive?

The procedure and strategies described in *Dynamic Read-Aloud Strategies for English Learners: Building Language and Literacy in the Primary Grades* were designed to respond to these questions—and to do so in a way that reflects the latest research in the field.

A Research-Based Approach

Research has identified many critical components of an effective, balanced literacy program for ELLs (August & Shanahan, 2006). Central to these components is the idea that if students are to build language and literacy skills they must connect with texts in meaningful, engaging, and purposeful ways.

The strategic read-aloud procedure we describe in this book provides an opportunity for students to do just that. What's more, the procedure is based on a theoretical framework made up of evidence-based research findings that addresses key elements of effective ELL programs. This chapter presents an overview of some of that research in an attempt to give readers the background information they need to understand the overarching framework behind strategic read-alouds as presented in this text.

We also describe how these research principles are incorporated into the design of the read-aloud strategies and procedures described in this book. Lastly, we visually depict the 10 steps involved in its design and implementation.

Forging Cultural Connections

According to Vygotsky (1978), learning takes place not in isolation but rather through social interaction dependent upon culture (i.e., as individuals interact within a social environment). His sociocultural theory contends that, in the initial stages of learning a skill, children attend and respond to adult modeling, teaching, and supportive encouragement. Over time, through varied means of adult encouragement and support—often referred to as *scaffolding* (Hobsbaum, Peters, & Sylva, 1996)—children develop the ability to use the skill independently and across contexts. The time between initial modeling of the skill by an adult or older, skilled child and the child's acquisition of and independent use of that skill, is referred to as the zone of proximal development (ZPD; Vygotsky, 1978).

With respect to ELLs, language and culture influence learning both prior to and during learning activities within the student's ZPD (Newman, Griffin, & Cole, 1989). Children are *enculturated* (Gudykunst & Kim, 1997), or socialized, into the beliefs, values, and behaviors of a particular culture by that culture's elders—typically parents, other significant adults, or community leaders (Moll, 1994). In this way, children acquire much of what they know about the world and others through their cultural experiences and interactions, which of course vary among cultural communities and groups (Moll, 1994). They also learn particular ways of thinking about the world and others through this process of enculturation. In order for effective learning to take place, then, it must tap into the knowledge children gain through social and cultural experiences, as well as align with the way children think about the world and their expectations for acquiring new knowledge. This is best achieved through teachers' connections to and deep understanding of the culture of the child's family and community.

Moving From the Familiar to the Unknown

Vygotsky contends that learning is facilitated when there are connections forged between home (the familiar) and school (the unknown; Meacham, 2001). He asserts, for example, that reading comprehension is dependent upon a student's ability to draw parallels between the content of a book and knowledge previously gained via one's home or cultural connections. As a result, readers need opportunities to identify what is "culturally familiar within [a] culturally different" context—in other words, they must be able to connect the realm of the familiar to the unfamiliar to increase understanding (Meacham, 2001, p. 192). Consequently, effective reading comprehension instruction might focus initially on helping students understand text about familiar concepts that originate in the context of the student's life at home; in the long term, instruction might focus on teaching students to generalize from that kind of familiar context to multiple contexts.

The concept of moving from the familiar to the unfamiliar also defines how ELLs acquire word meanings and, ultimately, new knowledge and concepts in both their primary and secondary languages. According to Nagy (1988), knowledge is structured through relationships; students understand new information by relating it to what they already know—the familiar. Therefore, teaching vocabulary so that ELLs see relationships between sets of words and concepts helps them understand and remember new ideas and acquire new language.

Still, many teachers find vocabulary instruction challenging, not only because is it difficult to identify which words are most important to teach but also because it is difficult to implement effective vocabulary instruction that encourages the development of deep and meaningful understanding of words, their connotations, and their uses across varied contexts.

Bridging Experience and New Learning

Research has found that a strategic read-aloud procedure is an effective way to develop the oral language, vocabulary, and listening comprehension skills of primary-grade children, in part because pre- and postreading activities can be designed to effectively connect learning with their past experiences (Vaughn, Linan-Thompson et al., 2006; Vaughn, Mathes et al., 2006). In fact, activities that "require students to reconstruct the story or make connections to life experiences" (Morrow & Brittain, 2003, p. 142) seem to be particularly beneficial in helping students gain vocabulary and comprehend text.

Such activities include discussions about the text the teacher plans to read aloud that activate prior knowledge about its content and make connections to that content in ways that promote inferential thinking. For instance, teachers commonly use statements like, "Tell me what you know about this...." to discern students' prior knowledge about a particular subject before they begin reading. Teachers can also connect prior knowledge with new learning after students have listened to the text by asking students if they have ever had an experience or feeling like that of one of the characters; to draw connections, comparisons, or contrasts between the events in the text and events in their own lives; or to cite similarities or differences between the text and other texts they have heard or read.

Accordingly, the process of choosing interesting and engaging texts for strategic read-aloud lessons is integral to the process of establishing links between students' backgrounds and new learning. The importance of ensuring that such texts are also culturally and experientially meaningful is discussed in detail in Chapter 2.

First-Language Literacy

In addition to advocating for instruction that is responsive to a student's sociocultural background, research also supports instruction in his or her native language whenever possible. Important considerations relative to native language literacy include the following:

- Most young children are experienced users of language. Their language has been acquired in the context of their homes and communities and within diverse cultural and linguistic settings. Their understanding of language, their language skills, and the way they use language have all been acquired in interactions using their native language.

- Experiences with their own language allow children to develop phonemic awareness and other oral language skills, predictors of later reading success (August & Shanahan, 2008; Snow, Burns, & Griffin, 1998).

- The amount of formal schooling a child receives in his or her first language is "the most powerful variable" in second-language learning (Collier, 1995, p. 23). Children are more likely to become readers and writers of English when they already have a strong foundation in their native language (August, 2002).

- Research has found that in the United States ELLs who (a) have no prior, formal literacy in their first language and (b) participate in programs in which English is the only language of instruction, typically will require 7–10 years or more to reach the same age and grade-level norms of their native English-speaking peers (Collier, 1995).

Although a discussion of the larger context of "bilingual versus English-language only" programs in U.S. public schools is beyond the scope of this book (and in some ways tangential to the purpose for which it is written), a summary of the current research and thinking in the field is offered to provide the context for the strategies we present. There is much research evidence (see August et al., 2008, for a detailed and comprehensive summary of empirical research in this area) citing the "better performance" of language-minority students who receive instruction in their native language (primarily Spanish) while also acquiring English when compared to "language-minority students instructed only in their second language (English)" (Snow, 2008, p. 285). However, researchers characterize that difference in performance as "moderate," noting that ELLs receiving instruction solely in English do, in fact, achieve in areas where that instruction is effective. They also contend that such students should be held to the same high level of expectations with respect to learning as their counterparts in bilingual programs.

In bilingual communities and contexts, the advantages of being bilingual are clearly noted. In such cases, the political climate and the availability of appropriate personnel and other resources may "favor providing bilingual instruction" with "no evidence-based disadvantages" (Snow, 2008, p. 285). In some communities and schools, however, due to a lack of personnel and resources, prevailing community politics, or the varied and diverse language backgrounds of ELLs, instruction is feasible only in English. Yet in both of these situations the most important predictor of positive learning outcomes is the quality of instruction students receive. What's more, no matter which instructional approach they take, teachers must understand and value the sociocultural context that affects their students' learning and respect parents' preferences for their children's language development. Only then will they be in a position to help their students become successful members of their home and school communities (Collier, 1995).

The strategic read-aloud activities described in this text were created in both English and Spanish for use with small groups of children in grades 1–3. The children were taught in the language of their core literacy program. For example, ELLs who were receiving their classroom literacy instruction in English participated in English read-aloud activities to develop oral language, vocabulary, and comprehension in English. Those ELLs who were receiving classroom literacy instruction in Spanish, through bilingual programs, participated in Spanish read-aloud activities to develop oral language, vocabulary, and comprehension in Spanish.

Thus, the same activities used to develop vocabulary and comprehension in the first language also can be used effectively with students in developing a second language—as long as teachers attend to the specialized needs of second-language learners. Furthermore, even when teaching in English, a teacher can clarify, if possible, key concepts or vocabulary in a student's native language as needed. For example, a teacher might explain an unfamiliar academic term such as *entire* to students in their native language to ensure that they fully comprehend its meaning and use.

Assessing Language Proficiency

Being able to accurately assess students' language skills and knowing how to help them gain language proficiency is the bedrock of ELL instruction. Language proficiency can be measured and assessed in both formal and informal ways, ranging from standardized tests to classroom-based assessments in the form of rubrics, state standards, or performance-based assessments. Teachers also discern ELLs language skills by (a) observing and recording examples of language use; (b) asking parents to describe their children's use of their native language and the amount of English-language exposure they have in the community; (c) meeting with an ESL specialist to discuss a student's formal language proficiency assessment scores and skill levels, informal measures of language development, and benchmark language behaviors; and (d) consulting district or state guides on student language proficiency levels and benchmark skills.

According to the research, teachers must be aware of students' language proficiency and literacy levels to effectively differentiate instruction in the areas of vocabulary and listening comprehension. This is true whether instruction is carried out in the student's first or second (or other) language (August & Hakuta, 1997; August & Shanahan, 2006; Cummins, 1994).

Developing Language Proficiency

It is important to remember that the development of oral proficiency and other measures of linguistic competence in a second language take place in much the same way as in a first language (Collier, 1995). That is to say, in both first- and second-language development, individuals initially spend time listening to the sounds of the new language. The goal is to become accustomed to (a) the language's tones, and how, when, and for what purpose they are used; and (b) specific words, phrases, and patterns of words used in interactions. Next, individuals begin to experiment and take risks with the new language by using it independently to communicate wants, needs, and ideas; one- and two-word phrases are used initially, followed by increasingly longer and more complex phrases and sentences as language development occurs over time. Two key language skills that should emerge during this development are language *flexibility*—which is the ability to say what one wants to say using one's own words rather than mimicking or repeating the words of others—and *elaboration*—which is the ability to verbally clarify one's thinking or elaborate on one's ideas, either spontaneously or when asked to do so (Anderson & Roit, 1996).

Although there are identifiable levels of language development (Krashen & Terrell, 1983; Tabors, 1997), the time it takes to advance within and through each level varies for first-language learning based on individual differences. The same is true of learning a second language, in part because some second-language learners, depending upon their age and level of cognitive development, have already developed many language skills in their first language. For bilingual students who have been taught to communicate in two languages simultaneously, perhaps since birth, the language development process differs somewhat to facilitate acquisition of two languages at the same time.

August and Shanahan (2008) point out that one key difference between the development of language and literacy in one's first language and one's second language is that

> Second-language learners have an additional set of intervening influences—those related to first-language literacy and oral proficiency...[there is] ample research evidence that certain aspects of second-language literacy development

are related to performance on similar constructs in the first language; this suggest that common underlying abilities play a significant role in both first- and second-language development.... Well developed literacy skills in the first language can facilitate second-language literacy development. (pp. 7–8)

To develop oral language proficiency in a second language, students must have opportunities to use that language for varied purposes (Chamot & O'Malley, 1994) with structured practice (August & Hakuta, 1997). For example, they should have a chance to learn—explicitly and through practical activities— how to use language to describe, request, convey information, ask questions, summarize, compare, justify, negotiate, and persuade. Moreover, they should be given varied opportunities to use these skills in the context of structured guidance and practice with different types of individuals (friends, those in authority, those with whom one is familiar and unfamiliar) and in different types of settings (one-on-one, small group, large group, familiar, unfamiliar, formal, informal). Such an approach ensures a depth and breadth of language learning and familiarity with the full range of pragmatic linguistic interaction.

During strategic read-aloud lessons, teachers regularly model proficient, fluent oral language as they read aloud to their students. Furthermore, structured class discussions and vocabulary activities provide opportunities for students to practice language production and explore varied contexts and purposes for word use. Teachers are encouraged to scaffold their instruction based on their knowledge of the continuum of oral language proficiency skills and their familiarity with the oral language skills of individual students in their class.

Figure 1 provides an informal overview of the stages of language development as an orientation to ways in which the strategic read-aloud procedure can be tailored to meet the language acquisition and learning needs of ELLs at three different levels of language proficiency (Krashen & Terrell, 1983; Ramsey, 1987; Southern California Comprehensive Assistance Center, 1998; Tabors, 1997).

Lastly, it is important to note that although language proficiency develops in a relatively predictable fashion, it occurs in response to the appropriateness and effectiveness of the learning environment and to factors related to individual learning style and language background (August & Hakuta, 1997; August & Shanahan, 2006). As a result, teachers must consider factors ranging from students' literacy levels in their first language to their cognitive ability, age at time of second-language learning, and sociocultural background when selecting texts and designing activities to use in strategic read-aloud lessons aimed at developing vocabulary acquisition and listening comprehension.

Figure 1. Levels of Language Proficiency: Implications for Strategic Read-Aloud Lessons

Levels of language proficiency: Implications for strategic read-alouds

Preproduction

- This is a silent period, lasting a few weeks to a few months for ELLs.

- Students observe and learn about phonology, syntax, semantics, and pragmatics of the new language.

Early language production

- Students begin to use short words, phrases, and labels to communicate.

- Students make more sophisticated attempts to communicate. The use of longer phrases and sentences signals the transition into intermediate fluency.

Intermediate and advanced fluency

- Students exhibit more complex word use and sentence structure, language flexibility, elaboration, and higher level skills such as analyzing, justifying, and expression opinions.

- Students use oral communication for varied purposes and have extended discussions with others.

- Students use higher-level communication.

Strategic read-aloud

Association of spoken words with pictures (if picture books are used), acquisition of learning syntax, rhythm, and phonology of the new language

Strategic read-aloud

Development of contextual and content-specific vocabulary

Reinforcement of comprehension with respect to varied forms and uses of language

Increased listening comprehension skills and ability to communicate in multiple ways for different purposes

Strategic read-aloud

Opportunities for students to transfer vocabulary acquisition across texts and contexts

Use of more complex texts, requiring the development and use of more complex comprehension skills and higher-level academic vocabulary

Note. From Krasher & Terrell, 1983; Ramsey, 1987; Southern California Comprehensive Assistance Center, 1998; Tabors, 1997.

Maximizing Comprehensible Input

One of the most important ways teachers meet the language needs of ELLs, no matter what their level of language development, is to scaffold their instruction to provide students with a maximum amount of what researchers call *comprehensible input* (Krashen, 1985, 1989). According to Gersten, Baker, and Marks (1999), teachers provide comprehensible input when they use words and language structures in ways that are both clear enough for students to understand and challenging enough to ensure that they learn new language.

Providing comprehensible input, because it stresses understanding and meaning-making, also involves the following:

> Presentation of background and context, explanation and rewording of unclear content, and the use of...context or visual cues.... When input is comprehensible, students understand most aspects of what is required for learning, and the learning experience pushes them to greater understanding. (Gersten, Baker, & Marks, 1999, p. 7)

One way teachers can maximize comprehensible input during strategic read-aloud lessons is by choosing vocabulary words to teach based on students' individual oral language and listening comprehension levels. For example, teachers may choose to teach a lower-level, functional vocabulary word such as *save* to students with lower levels of proficiency while teaching the word *store* (meaning *to save up*) to students with higher levels of proficiency who already understand the meaning of the word *save*.

Language Acquisition vs. Language Learning

Krashen (1985) distinguishes between two complementary means of developing competence in a second language: acquisition and learning. Language acquisition involves the "subconscious process" of developing competence in a language; a student informally, and often without conscious awareness, develops understanding of word meanings, ways in which words and phrases are used, and the forms of language used in different situations with different people.

However, such information can also be formally and explicitly taught. In such cases, language develops consciously and as such is the basis for second-language learning. Through the use of explicit instruction, for example, teachers can give students opportunities to make meaningful connections between words, concepts, and the contexts in which they are used (Au, 1993; Barrera, 1992; García, Montes, Janisch, Bouchereau, & Consalvi, 1993).

It has been argued (Krashen, 1985) that instructional environments that promote natural language acquisition are often preferable to those focusing exclusively on direct, explicit teaching of grammatical structures and "rules" associated with language learning. However, other research (e.g., Chamot & O'Malley, 1994; Ellis, 1990) supports the notion of allowing students opportunities to acquire language through natural and authentic learning activities and interactions along with explicit instruction focused on formal language structures, forms, and uses.

An example of how second-language skills are acquired during strategic read-aloud lessons would include the incidental learning of word meanings and language patterns as students listen to a story being read aloud. Explicit instruction, on the other hand, can be delivered as part of the read-aloud experience through the structured and purposeful use of several best practice, evidence-based strategies. Those include (a) clearly communicating objectives to students so that they are aware of the important elements to attend to during the lesson (Southern California Comprehensive Assistance Center, 1998), (b) targeting comprehension by activating existing knowledge related to a text before it is read and through explicit discussion of the ideas in the text and the application of those ideas to students' own experiences after it is read (Grabe, 1991), and (c) teaching vocabulary words explicitly either prior to or following the reading of a text (Grabe, 1991).

By structuring the read-aloud experience in ways that not only support second-language acquisition but also provide explicit instruction that allows for second-language vocabulary and comprehension learning, teachers create opportunities for students to expand their language understanding and skill in multiple and varied ways. For example, as students discuss the texts read aloud, they draw on their knowledge of formal and informal language while incorporating the use of new language skills.

Interpersonal vs. Academic Language

Researchers in the field of second-language acquisition typically distinguish interpersonal language proficiency (language used to conversationally communicate with others) from academic language proficiency (formal language used in textbooks). Table 1 compares these two types of language proficiency and describes ways that each is developed through strategic read-aloud lessons.

Critical to the development of both types of language proficiency is the amount of contextual support afforded a student during a specific language exchange—or conversation. That support could come in the form of (a) visuals such as pictures, graphic organizers, or other types of media designed to help clarify key vocabulary or content; (b) gesturing or movement used to enhance

Table 1. Interpersonal and Academic Language Proficiency

Language proficiency type	Description	As used in strategic read-aloud lessons
Interpersonal Language Proficiency (Cummins, 1984; Scarcella, 2003)	Typically includes conversational skills (pragmatics, grammar) learned through informal social interactions in environments in which students receive contextualized language support	Students discuss and relate prior experiences to information in the text both before and after it is read aloud.
Academic Language Proficiency (Cummins, 1984; Scarcella, 2003)	Typically demands more cognitively demanding, advanced language skills involving complex sentence structures and higher-level vocabulary that is often less contextualized Mastery requires "extensive knowledge of the vocabulary of everyday, ordinary situations" (Scarcella, 2003, p. 28) acquired through social interactions in which academic language is used to communicate	Students are provided with multiple opportunities to learn, use, and generalize academic vocabulary. Students are taught concrete representations of concepts. Students take part in multiple and varied activities and opportunities featuring authentic, real-life experiences related to such vocabulary and concepts.

meaning and understanding; and (c) linguistic emphasis (varied intonation, stress, repetition) on particular words, phrases, or content to highlight, emphasize, and clarify their use within specific phrases or contexts. The more contextual support provided, the easier it is for students to understand and master the type of language used in a specific exchange (Cummins, 1984, 1994; Edelsky, 1990).

Research has shown that with proper support, students can typically achieve effective interpersonal language proficiency within the first few years of language study. To achieve proficiency equal to that of a native speaker in academic language, on the other hand, typically takes 5–10 years, even with effective support (Collier, 1987, 1989).

Strategically embedding language development, vocabulary, and comprehension skill development into strategic read-aloud lessons helps develop both the interpersonal and the academic language proficiency of ELLs. However, given the need for ELLs to efficiently and effectively develop the academic proficiency necessary to access content area texts and to reach high levels of academic achievement, more emphasis is dedicated in this book to describing how teachers can strategically plan and implement instruction that targets the development of their students' academic language proficiency.

One way strategic read-aloud lessons help build academic language is through activities that scaffold instruction in content area literacy (Brinton, Snow, & Wesche, 1993; Scarcella, 2003). For example, teachers can make content area vocabulary words used in science or social studies texts more comprehensible to students through instruction that focuses on the way language and vocabulary words are structured, a process described in Chapter 3. In addition, texts used for read-alouds can be grouped by themes related to specific content areas. Examples of content-related themes appropriate for the primary grades include families, pets, insects, and ocean animals. Teachers can then choose to teach vocabulary words from each text that are more content-specific, or academic, in nature.

Strategic Read-Aloud Lessons: Scope and Sequence

Figure 2 summarizes the easy-to-follow scope and sequence of the 10 steps involved in designing and carrying out the strategic read-aloud procedure described in this book, referencing at each step one or more of the critical components of an effective literacy program for ELLs discussed in this chapter. As stated earlier, Chapters 2–4 discuss each of these steps in detail, and Chapter 5 describes sample lessons that incorporate all of these elements.

Research to Practice: Reflecting on Teaching and Learning

1. Many states provide rubrics for informally evaluating the language proficiency levels of students in reading, writing, listening, and speaking and offer suggestions for instruction at each stage of mastery. Consult your state or district website for information that will help you determine the language proficiency level(s) of your students and effectively adapt instruction to enhance language development at their level(s).

2. Reflect on your previous experiences reading books aloud to ELLs. Which, if any, of the steps included in the strategic read-aloud procedure described so far in this book did you incorporate into the read-alouds you implemented? Compare and contrast the procedure you used with the intervention procedure presented here. What do you see as the benefits of

Figure 2. Overview of the Scope and Sequence of the Strategic Read-Aloud Procedure

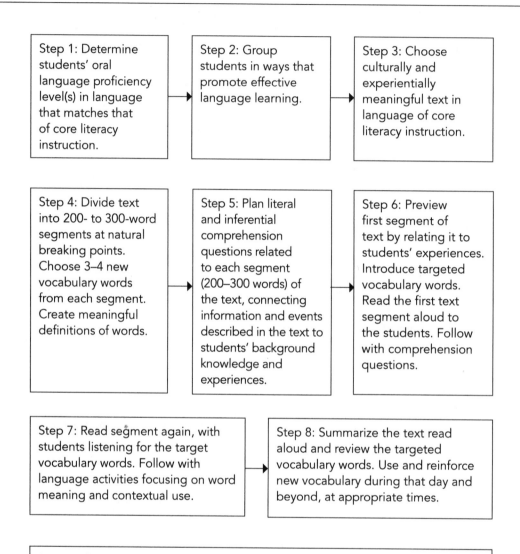

Step 1: Determine students' oral language proficiency level(s) in language that matches that of core literacy instruction.

Step 2: Group students in ways that promote effective language learning.

Step 3: Choose culturally and experientially meaningful text in language of core literacy instruction.

Step 4: Divide text into 200- to 300-word segments at natural breaking points. Choose 3–4 new vocabulary words from each segment. Create meaningful definitions of words.

Step 5: Plan literal and inferential comprehension questions related to each segment (200–300 words) of the text, connecting information and events described in the text to students' background knowledge and experiences.

Step 6: Preview first segment of text by relating it to students' experiences. Introduce targeted vocabulary words. Read the first text segment aloud to the students. Follow with comprehension questions.

Step 7: Read segment again, with students listening for the target vocabulary words. Follow with language activities focusing on word meaning and contextual use.

Step 8: Summarize the text read aloud and review the targeted vocabulary words. Use and reinforce new vocabulary during that day and beyond, at appropriate times.

Step 9: The next day, begin by reviewing text read on previous day and related vocabulary words. Then continue process, beginning again at Step 6.

Step 10: After the entire text has been read over a number of consecutive days, end by rereading the entire text. Engage students in activities that target 4–5 of the most challenging vocabulary words from the text. Begin again at Step 1 with a new text on the same theme or a new set of thematic texts the following day (Step 1).

modifying read-aloud activities in the ways suggested here? What do you see as the challenges?

3. Identify two of the concepts discussed in this chapter that you would like to learn more about in relation to implementing the strategic read-aloud procedure described thus far. Let these goals guide your reading of the remaining chapters of this book.

Suggested Readings for Further Study

Gottlieb, M. (2006). *Assessing English language learners: Bridges from language proficiency to academic achievement.* Thousand Oaks, CA: Corwin.

Hickman, P., Pollard-Durodola, S., and Vaughn, S. (2004). Storybook reading: Improving vocabulary and comprehension for English-language learners. *The Reading Teacher, 57*(8), 720–730.

Vaughn, S., Mathes, P.G., Linan-Thompson, S., and Francis, D.J. (2005). Teaching English language learners at risk for reading disabilities to read: Putting research into practice. *Learning Disabilities Research & Practice, 20*(1), 58–67. doi:10.1111/j.1540–5826.2005.00121.x

Strategic Read-Aloud Design: Grouping, Text Selection, and Building Content Knowledge

Mrs. Barnett:	(second-grade general education teacher) Today I am going to read aloud a book that will tell us a lot about spiders. The name of the book is Spiders. The author is a woman named Gail Gibbons. She has written a lot of books about the world around us. Since we've been talking about insects and other small creatures in our science lessons, I thought this book might help us learn more about spiders. Before I begin reading, let's think about what we already know about spiders.
David:	(a recent immigrant from Korea) Black. Brown.
Mrs. Barnett:	That's right, we know that some spiders are black and others are brown.
Kristina:	(a Mexican American ELL) A spider web is on my porch.
Mrs. Barnett:	Good thinking! Spiders like to spin silky webs. I wonder why they spin webs? Let's start reading to see if we can find out!

Mrs. Barnett is a monolingual, English-speaking teacher working in a suburban school district that has experienced an increase in ELL enrollment. Some of her students are recent immigrants; others represent the first and second generation of families who immigrated to the United States. Her goal is to make sure that she is using engaging materials written at an appropriate level of understanding for these students as well as for the English monolingual struggling readers—typically developing second graders—and advanced learners who are also in her class. Here, she works with a small group of ELLs, focusing on activating their prior knowledge of and experience with the topic of spiders and insects before she begins to read an informational text on the subject aloud to them. She knows such a move will give them access to vocabulary and concepts that will make the read-aloud experience more meaningful.

Armed with a foundational understanding of second-language acquisition principles and knowledge of their students' language proficiency levels and skills, teachers of ELLs are ready to begin creating dynamic and strategic read-aloud lessons to build vocabulary and comprehension. The first step is to set the stage by (a) grouping students for read-aloud lessons in ways that will promote effective language learning, (b) selecting texts to read aloud that not only generate interest in the read-aloud experience but also provide material that is both comprehensible and challenging, and (c) planning activities to use during the read-aloud process to activate and build ELLs' content knowledge.

These elements require specific attention to a research-based instructional design that meets the needs of language learners with diverse skills, backgrounds, and interests. Such a design is informed by the research findings and best practices of second-language acquisition and learning discussed in Chapter 1, with particular emphasis on the concept of instructional scaffolding (Vygotsky, 1978). Together, these elements provide a guide for designing effective read-aloud lessons for ELLs with respect to grouping, text selection, and content knowledge development.

Best-Practice Strategies

As discussed in Chapter 1, research on second-language learning specifies that knowing students' level of language proficiency is the first step in creating effective read-aloud lessons for ELLs. A number of best-practice strategies grounded in research can guide teachers through the next steps in the process: grouping students, selecting appropriate texts, and planning for effective content and language learning. Specifically, teachers are urged to

- Design read-aloud instruction for small groups of students, an approach shown to be particularly significant in improving language and literacy outcomes for ELLs who lag behind their peers in literacy development in English or Spanish (Linan-Thompson, Vaughn, Hickman, & Kouzekanani, 2003; Vaughn, Linan-Thompson et al., 2005; Vaughn, Linan-Thompson et al., 2006)
- Choose texts to read aloud that are meaningful and provide appropriate language input in terms of vocabulary level and complexity of text and syntactical structures (August, 2003)
- Select vocabulary words from texts for targeted instruction that are responsive to students' levels of language proficiency (Calderón et al., 2005)
- Modify speech and intonation when reading aloud to make language engaging and comprehensible, thereby scaffolding instruction to facilitate student learning (Chamot & O'Malley, 1994)
- Incorporate visuals and concrete objects, body language and gestures, drama, and other varied media to facilitate vocabulary acquisition and

comprehension in students who sometimes require instruction that represents abstract concepts in concrete ways (García et al., 1993)

- Encourage students to respond to questions and statements about interesting texts (Anderson & Roit, 1998; Au, 1993; Grabe, 1991) in their own words, thereby providing opportunities for them to experiment with new vocabulary and language structures (Anderson & Roit, 1998; Au, 1993; Chamot & O'Malley, 1994; Fitzgerald, 1995)
- Provide students with opportunities to actively participate in conversations using academic language as a way of building conceptual understanding and relating textual content to their own experiences (Scarcella, 2003)

Instructional Scaffolding During Read-Aloud Lessons

Instructional scaffolding refers to the assistance an adult gives to a child at his or her level of need in relation to their ability to access and accomplish a task (Vygotsky, 1978). This assistance is gradually reduced as the child becomes more competent and independent, yet it is flexible in its attention to multiple aspects of a student's learning and development, providing more support when needed and less as competence grows. According to Santamaría, Fletcher, and Bos (2002),

> Unlike rigid scaffolds used in the construction of a building, educational scaffolds are fluid, dynamic, and interactive. They can be used to temporarily assist both English language learners with learning disabilities and academically proficient students, as they develop knowledge, understanding, strategies, and skills. (p. 135)

There are three major types of instructional scaffolding—task, materials, and comprehensible input—that apply to working with ELLs in general and, specifically, to the read-aloud experience (Hogan & Pressley, 1997; Jiménez, Gersten, & Rivera, 1996; Kame'enui, Carnine, Dixon, Simmons, & Coyne, 2002; Santamaría, Fletcher, & Bos, 2002; Tabors, 1997).

Task scaffolding takes place when teachers provide students with support that helps them complete an activity. Examples of task scaffolding include monitoring students' independent work while providing them with one-on-one feedback and offering alternate explanations during a lesson when students become confused. Structured, cooperative grouping of students for an activity or assignment can also be considered a task scaffold. In such a setting both the teacher and the students themselves can provide opportunities for each member of the group to participate in ways that reflect their individual ability levels. Teachers gradually reduce the amount of support they provide as students become more independent in completing such activities.

Materials scaffolding refers to the choices teachers make with respect to the texts and other supplemental materials they use in the classroom. Such choices are made by selecting materials that are culturally and experientially relevant, thematically appropriate, and support students' learning by taking into account their language needs and areas of interest. Scaffolding instruction with respect to materials also includes the use of graphic organizers, which can be used to help students understand concepts, and sentence prompts or sentence frames, which encourage students' oral responses and, in turn, their oral language development.

Comprehensible input scaffolding occurs when teachers communicate with students in ways that students can understand but that also promote the learning of new material. Teachers vary their communication style and language use to both match and challenge the language proficiency levels of their students simultaneously.

As depicted in Table 2, instruction scaffolded in these three ways is integrated throughout the design of the strategic read-aloud procedure described in this book in order to maximize content and language learning opportunities for students. Note, too, how the procedure reflects the best-practice strategies discussed earlier.

Thus, instructional scaffolding—the use of a variety of task, materials, and comprehensible input supports teachers put in place to facilitate and extend student learning—is evident throughout the planning and implementation stages of the read-aloud procedure. This concept will be explored in greater detail in relation to each of the three elements of design planning (grouping, text selection, and content knowledge development) discussed in this chapter. Instructional scaffolding with respect to vocabulary and listening comprehension development will be taken up in Chapters 3 and 4.

Grouping Students for Effective Learning

Although strategic read-aloud lessons typically involve the entire class, research evidence suggests ELLs experience the best outcomes with respect to building language, vocabulary, and listening comprehension when they receive structured, high-quality instruction in small groups (Linan-Thompson et al., 2003; Meacham, 2003; Morrow & Brittain, 2003; Vaughn, Cirino, et al., 2006;

Table 2. Scaffolding the Read-Aloud Experience for ELLs

Type of scaffold	Use of scaffolds, best-practice strategies in read-aloud design
Task	• Create positive, culturally responsive relationships with and between students, thereby developing a community of learners and an environment in which students feel safe taking risks in learning language • Align lessons with student culture, experiential background, and interests • Group students in ways that maximize opportunities for language use and learning • Expand students' ideas and the language they use to express those ideas by rephrasing their responses in new and (if appropriate) more complex ways, thereby promoting language flexibility • Ask open-ended questions and providing prompts that encourage students to expand and elaborate on their ideas • Assist students who request clarification or further explanation, as needed • Encourage students to use new vocabulary words as they talk with one another in either their first or second language about texts read aloud • Provide students with positive, encouraging feedback
Materials	• Choose texts that reflect students' cultural and background experiences and interests that are written at appropriate language levels • Demonstrate key concepts using visuals, manipulatives, and other concrete objects as a way of increasing understanding • Design vocabulary and comprehension activities using graphic organizers, sentence frames, or other materials to support students' comprehension and use of new vocabulary words and to help students respond in their own words or with new syntax
Comprehensible input	• Choose vocabulary words and developing meanings based on students' language proficiency levels • Model fluent speaking, language flexibility, elaboration, and vocabulary use • Adjust speech and language structures to both match and extend students' vocabulary skills and language proficiency levels • Introduce new content in the students' primary language, if appropriate, and describing new concepts using familiar English vocabulary and syntax • Encourage students to actively self-monitor their comprehension and seek clarification when needed • Clarify student misunderstandings related to vocabulary and comprehension

Note. Compiled from Anderson & Roit, 1996, 1998; Au, 1993; Calderón et al, 2005; Chamot & O'Malley, 1994; Fitzgerald, 1995; García et al., 1993; Grabe, 1991; Hickman & Dray, 2007; Scarcella, 2003

Vaughn, Mathes et al., 2006). In fact, both literacy instruction in general (Lou, Spence, Pulsen, Chambers, & d'Apollonia, 1996) and specifically, instruction delivered through read-aloud lessons have been shown to be more effective when occurring with small groups of students than when in one-on-one settings or with larger groups (Blok, 1999; Morrow, 1987, 1988; Morrow & Smith, 1990). Such outcomes assume grouping practices that are sensitive to cultural nuances in interaction patterns. That is, students should be grouped in ways that maximize their willingness to contribute in relation to cultural and gender-based norms (Meacham, 2003).

Practically speaking, the benefits of working with three to four students at a time include increased opportunities for (a) teachers to target students' specific skill needs, (b) students to be engaged in the text, and (c) teachers to assist students in building language skills by giving them more opportunities to respond and receive feedback while talking about books. In small groups, teachers are also better able to scaffold their instruction by gearing their interactions with individual students, whether in the primary or secondary language, to each student's oral language level (Vaughn & Linan-Thompson, 2003; Vaughn, Linan-Thompson, & Hickman, 2003).

Class Management of Small-Group Read-Aloud Sessions

Conducting strategic read-aloud sessions with small groups of students requires careful planning in terms of classroom and instructional time management, particularly for teachers in self-contained, general education classrooms. Some creative options might include scheduling such sessions while students are rotating through learning centers, reading or working independently on content area activities, or taking part in peer collaboration activities such as partnered reading. Small-group read-alouds can also be scheduled during instructional periods when there is a reading specialist or other support personnel in the classroom.

Homogeneous Grouping

Consideration of the relative merits of homogeneous versus heterogeneous grouping of students should also be taken into account. Each affords benefits. When a small group includes students who are all functioning at a similar level of language proficiency, the read-aloud experience can be designed to target a single set of vocabulary words that all of the students find challenging without being frustrating. Likewise, a teacher can use the same comprehension questions and related activities to meet the needs of all students in the group if their skill levels are similar. For example, teachers working with a small group of students with higher levels of language proficiency can use the read-aloud session as an opportunity for targeting higher-level thinking skills.

Heterogeneous Grouping

Heterogeneous grouping has the advantage of exposing students to varied levels of vocabulary. In such a setting, students have the opportunity to work at higher levels than might be the case in a group of peers with similar proficiency levels. It also gives advanced students the opportunity to help their peers by modeling more highly developed language skills.

Furthermore, heterogeneous grouping across language proficiency levels allows for differentiation by interests or by background knowledge. For example, during a thematic unit on mammals, students—regardless of their language proficiency levels—may choose to join either a small group studying dogs or one studying whales. Often, ELLs are able to comprehend higher levels of text if it pertains to a subject in which they are interested or have background knowledge (Anderson & Roit, 1996). In such cases, heterogeneous grouping may provide greater opportunity for language and vocabulary development.

Disadvantages to heterogeneous grouping include the possibility that, given the range of students' language proficiency levels, the vocabulary and comprehension activities will be either too easy or too difficult for some students. Such a situation may reduce students' engagement, understanding, and potential for optimal learning. It can also be ineffective. Instead of learning four new vocabulary words during a read-aloud session, a student may only learn one. For example, if the text is insufficiently challenging, the student may already have known one word, or if it is too difficult technically or conceptually the student may not be able to grasp its meaning. This is most likely to occur when the heterogeneous groups are made up of students with particularly diverse learning levels.

Heterogeneous grouping may also make it difficult for a teacher to find books that are neither too easy nor too difficult, in terms of comprehensible input, for some students in the group. In this case, however, other elements of the read-aloud experience, such as comprehension and vocabulary activities, can be differentiated to align with each individual student's level of oral language proficiency.

Selecting Texts

Text selection is a vital part of instructional scaffolding of the read-aloud process. Research clearly stresses the importance of providing ELLs with high-quality texts—works of fiction (e.g., narratives) with engaging storylines, and nonfictional, informational, expository works written in academic language—that are written at appropriate levels and tap into their experiential and cultural backgrounds (Anderson & Roit, 1996). Figure 3 graphically depicts elements that should be taken into consideration when choosing texts for strategic read-aloud activities. Each will be described in detail in the section that follows.

Figure 3. Characteristics of Texts Chosen for Strategic Read-Alouds With ELLs

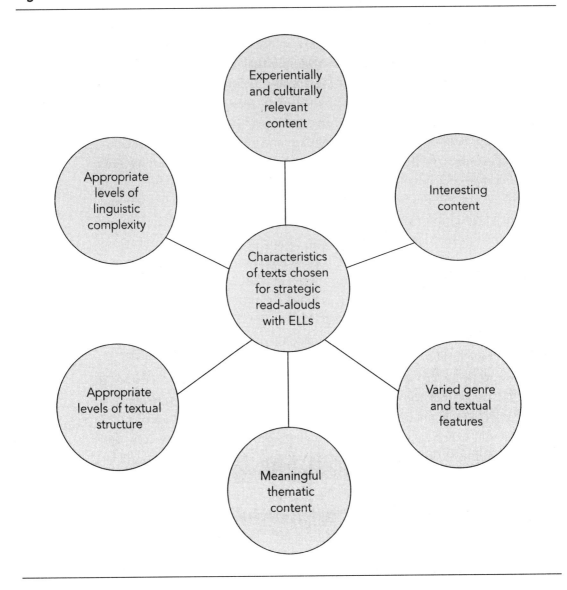

Experientially and Culturally Relevant Content

For a text—whether narrative or expository—to be truly culturally and experientially relevant to a group of students, it should provide more than just representations of characters who are similar to them in ethnicity and race. Instead, both its contents and context should reflect characters, settings, situations, behaviors, and values with which the students are likely to be familiar (Anderson & Roit, 1996). In such cases, students more often "identify with the text, react to the text, and connect text to prior knowledge" in their discussions, which in turn boosts comprehension (Anderson & Roit, p. 305).

Consider a number of popular children's picture books that do just that. *Chicken Sunday* by Patricia Polacco centers on a diverse community in which a group of African American children decide to work together to earn money to buy a special gift for a neighbor, Miss Eula. After a misunderstanding occurs, the community comes together to celebrate their diversity. Many children from a variety of ethnic and cultural backgrounds can relate to the events, friendships, and rich community diversity depicted in this book. In this sense, it could be considered an experientially relevant text.

Likewise, *Julius, the Baby of the World* by Kevin Henkes (also available in Spanish) centers on a character's feelings about and interactions with her new baby brother. This may be a relevant text for many students who have experienced the arrival of a younger sibling and how such an event changes family dynamics. Although the arrival of a younger sibling may be perceived differently in different cultures (less positively in individualistic cultures in which one's individual standing is considered important than in collectivistic cultures that place higher relative value on group membership and harmony), it is still an experience to which many students can relate.

Yet another example is *A Chair for My Mother* by Vera B. Williams. The story, set in an urban environment, is about a child who lives with her mother and grandmother and wants to buy a special present for her mother. Clearly, there are themes explored in this book—living in an extended family, wanting to do kind things for others—that are relevant to many students' lives.

Interesting Content

In the words of Mary Lee Hahn (2002), "Every year, a unique community of distinct individuals fills your classroom…. Who your students are should play a huge part in the books you choose to read to them" (p. 28). As they design read-aloud lessons, teachers need to keep Hahn's words in mind and carefully consider not only their students' cultural and experiential backgrounds but also their developmental and intellectual interests.

For example, students in the primary grades often find works of fiction relating to families, friendships, home, school, and community events particularly engaging and interesting largely because such topics reflect events in their own lives. Nonfiction books of interest to children in the primary grades include those that focus on topics such as neighborhood and community, insect and animal families, ecosystems, planets and the solar system, weather, magnets, plants, and other aspects of the natural world. (Many books by Gail Gibbons cover such topics in engaging and interesting ways.)

Engaging works that bring math concepts and vocabulary to life include *The Doorbell Rang* by Pat Hutchins, *One Hundred Hungry Ants* by Elinor J. Pinczes, and *Spaghetti and Meatballs for All* by Marilyn Burns.

Varied Genre and Textual Features

It is important for teachers to read widely and peruse a variety of high-quality texts from multiple sources before making final decisions about which ones best lend themselves to strategic read-aloud sessions. They also need to ensure that the choices they make include not only works of narrative fiction but also nonfiction, informational texts. Researchers have determined that reading narrative stories to students does not adequately prepare them to read and understand non-narrative text (Smolkin & Donovan, 2000). In addition, the use of nonfiction, informational texts in the primary grades can be especially helpful when it comes to strengthening students' vocabulary, expanding their knowledge, and increasing their familiarity with varied text structures (Duke, 1999, 2000; Duke, Bennett-Armistead, & Roberts, 2003; Teale, 2003).

Yet evidence continues to suggest that most children lack exposure to informational text (Duke, 2000; Moss, 2004)—not because children are disinterested in informational texts; in fact, quite the opposite is true. Students enjoy informational texts about topics they consider interesting and relevant, such as their own natural and experiential worlds and new worlds and ideas. The same guidelines that apply to selecting narrative texts apply to selecting informational texts. Appropriate texts reflect students' interests, expand their world knowledge, and cover a wide range of linguistic complexity. In the recent past, the availability and quality of information texts has increased significantly; many make terrific choices for strategic read-aloud lessons.

Teachers also need to provide opportunities for their students to be exposed to a wide range of literary genres, particularly in the realm of informational text, because reading across genres is critical if students are to develop an understanding of the varied purposes and uses of literacy and language. For that reason, teachers should incorporate not just books but also newspapers, magazines, poetry, and riddles into the read-aloud experience. All offer important learning opportunities for ELLs while simultaneously helping teachers tap into a wide range of students' literacy interests (August & Shanahan, 2006; Teale, 2003).

Meaningful Thematic Content

Thematic teaching allows students to gain deep conceptual knowledge as new information acquired over time is used to strengthen existing knowledge and understanding (Hirsch, 2006). By using an integrated approach to delivering curriculum, the teacher also provides opportunities for students to learn concepts and use skills across content areas in broad and meaningful ways. Thus, thematic read-alouds have the potential not only to link multiple books by content for a series of read-aloud sessions but also to provide multiple opportunities for adding depth and breadth to student knowledge, understanding, and learning.

Both informational and narrative texts can and should be used in read-aloud sessions to integrate content area learning with language arts through thematic units in the primary grades. Such sessions can be a powerful part of content area teaching in that they offer students support for comprehension through (a) an examination of different types of text structures (e.g., sequenced events, comparison and contrast, topic sentence and supporting details) and (b) exposure to new or contrasting (e.g., fact versus fictional representation) perspectives related to content. Texts used in these ways build conceptual knowledge and linguistic skills simultaneously, serving to strengthen the academic language skills of ELLs that are so critical to their success.

Appropriate Levels of Text Structure

When choosing a text to use with ELLs, it is also important to consider the organizational patterns that make up the text's internal structure. Different text structures are read aloud in different ways depending on whether a teacher's goal is to highlight content or familiarize students with the features of different types and genre of texts.

Narrative texts are designed to entertain the reader by telling stories that include structural elements such as an introduction, a challenge or conflict, and a resolution. Characters, plot, setting, and theme are other critical elements inherent in narrative fiction. Typically, teachers use narratives to reinforce comprehension strategies such as retelling, sequencing, summarizing, predicting, and questioning. Because narratives tend to be structured in a fairly natural, straightforward way and often include elements of plot, character, and theme that are identifiable to and resonate with students, such texts are often easier for students to comprehend than informational texts.

Informational, or expository, texts are typically less linear in structure and format than narratives. Once in a while, narratives will include elements of structural complexity, such as flashbacks, dream sequences, and shifts in character perspective, as well as elements of nonlinear formatting, such as speech bubbles. However, it is typically informational texts that are most likely to use text blocks, labels, charts, graphs, and other graphic organizers that highlight material in nonlinear ways.

For example, a single page from a book on ocean mammals may contain 8–10 illustrated blocks of informational text related to the main topic of whales. Although all the information presented is related, the order in which it is presented on the page or read is not vital to comprehension. A reader can proceed in a clockwise or counterclockwise direction, or randomly; a linear or logical approach is not necessary.

"Organizational devices" (Lapp, Flood, Brock, and Fischer, 2007, p. 220) that affect the way written and graphic material is formatted, or arranged on a page, can also reinforce comprehension skills. For example, titles, headings, and short paragraphs, all of which are typical elements of expository texts, can help clarify the relationship between a main idea and its supporting details. Visual representation of content, in the form of such elements as pull-out charts, labels, and graphs, often highly engaging and dramatic, can also deepen students' understanding of concepts such as comparison and contrast and cause and effect.

Furthermore, because the purpose of expository writing is to describe, inform, and explain, expository texts typically include numerous signal, or cue, words (e.g., *first, next, last, because, like, therefore*) designed to alert students to the structure of the text in ways that promote comprehension. Because attending to signal words is an important comprehension strategy, teachers should find explicit ways to teach such words to ELLs (Vacca & Vacca, 2008). On the other hand, expository text can also include very specific and highly technical vocabulary (e.g., Tier III words as described in Chapter 3) that teachers may choose not to teach explicitly. Typically, such words are understood due to how they are used in context.

Appropriate Levels of Linguistic Complexity

Lastly, teachers seeking texts that will actively engage ELLs and motivate them to acquire academic language skills need to take into account a text's linguistic complexity. When selecting texts for strategic read-aloud sessions with ELLs, it is generally a good idea to choose texts written at one to two grade levels above the students' grade placement; in this way, students are exposed not only to challenging vocabulary but also to text structures and elements of linguistic complexity that will increase their understanding of academic language. A text's linguistic complexity refers to several factors, including the following:

- The vocabulary level at which the text is written
- The variety of verb tenses and how often and in what contexts changes in verb tense occur
- The use of complex figures of speech, such as idiomatic expressions, analogies, similes, metaphors, onomatopoeia, and personification
- The complexity of syntax and semantic features, such as sentence structure and length, as well as the presence of dialogue in the text
- The extent to which a text includes implicit language that requires readers to draw pragmatic inferences in order to decipher meaning
- The complexity of a text's morphology, or word forms

A good rule of thumb is that the level of text complexity should be challenging for students—but not beyond their understanding—and within the conceptual frame of their ZPD (Vygotsky, 1978; see Chapter 1). Texts that are too long or have too many words or sentences on a page should be avoided. (Ideally, texts used for read-alouds are structured so that they can be broken into 200- to 250-word passages and read easily over a period of four or five days.) Likewise, texts with too many unfamiliar words, figures of speech, or overly complex sentences or ideas may detract from students' comprehension and understanding of words in context.

As for vocabulary, the goal of a strategic read-aloud lesson is to expose students to vocabulary levels that foster language skills and proficiency and develop academic language related to content. This issue will be explored at length in Chapter 3.

Often, teachers find themselves facing a class of students who exhibit a wide range of language-proficiency levels. In such cases, activities related to the teaching of comprehension can and should be differentiated. Even if the linguistic complexity of a given text is slightly below some students' ZPD they can be asked comprehension questions that require them to use higher-level comprehension skills. Such questions, for example, could focus on how the events in the text reflect the students' own lives or feelings or how they think the characters might be feeling. Answering questions of this nature requires students to draw inferences. Students might also be asked to summarize the events or main idea of a passage, a task that requires complex comprehension skills.

It should be noted that there are times when curricular expectations influence text selection. Some school districts, for example, issue curriculum matrices that dictate specific texts teachers must use—and in what order and on which days they must use them. In such cases, teachers may have little, if any, flexibility with respect to using supplementary or substitute texts. Still, whether mandated or teacher-selected, texts should offer students opportunities to engage actively with material that draws on students' experiences, offers comprehensible input and support for language and content learning, and reflects appropriate levels of text structures and linguistic complexity.

Drawing On and Building Conceptual Knowledge

Hirsch (2006) argues that, without broad knowledge, children will have difficulty comprehending text. Neglecting to build knowledge contributes to inequity in our school systems and fuels the achievement gap between those who are poor and those who are not. In effect, those who are proficient in language understanding will gain in language proficiency while those who lack such understanding will continue to fall further and further behind (Hirsch). This statement has profound implications when considered within the context of the diversity that exists among language learners in terms of their prior background experiences.

For students, including ELLs, to comprehend text that is read aloud, they must, to some degree, be familiar with the situations or realities that are described in the text. They must also be interested in and clear about the relevance of learning more about those situations or realities. Hirsch (2006) suggests that broad knowledge in the realm of culture and environmental experience are prerequisites to gaining deeper understanding from listening to or reading text. The term *schema* is often used to refer to cognitive frameworks that represent known concepts, meaning that for many everyday experiences, individuals develop an understanding of the whole of that experience, which is then used as a base upon which to build new knowledge. For example, many people have a schema, or understanding of what it means to go to a bookstore, order pizza, or get directions to the library.

Similarly, teachers have a schema for effective teaching, or what good instruction looks like, sounds like, and feels like. When they engage in professional development sessions, attend workshops, or read professional journal articles or books related to effective teaching, they activate their prior understanding of effective teaching; new information gained builds on that understanding, increasing content knowledge and expanding the conceptual framework—or schema—related to that content.

The same process occurs when students listen to texts being read aloud. In other words, as discussed in Chapter 1, the more they are able to draw parallels between the known and the unknown—the familiar and unfamiliar—the greater the likelihood that they will understand the text. If students already have some knowledge or experience related to the ideas and concepts in the text, they are often able to draw parallels from memory. And with a working understanding of the topic, they can more easily acquire new facts and infer information from the text, adding to their already existing schema.

If students have not had experiences with the content, then they must build new frameworks, or schema, related to the information in the text. This is also true when it comes to students' knowledge and understanding of language and text structures. Students who have had instruction in or experiences with different text structures and comprehension strategies typically develop a schema for those structures and strategies. As a result, they are able to apply them—albeit initially with assistance—to comprehending new text.

Creating opportunities for students to access and share their prior knowledge about the topic or text structure of a read-aloud selection before it is read aloud gives the teacher information that can be used to determine how to scaffold instruction related to developing students' language and comprehension skills. Then, as they listen to the book being read aloud over the course of several days, students are able to broaden their schema with regard to content knowledge and text structure, which in turn increases their understanding of the text. Listening to a book read in short sections over time allows language instruction to be delivered in manageable chunks. For example, students are only required to learn an appropriate number of new vocabulary words at once. It also gives students opportunities to review what was learned over several days in relation to a consistent text and is an efficient way to solidify learning and help connect new understanding to prior knowledge. This is particularly critical for ELLs who are receiving literacy instruction exclusively in English and who may need additional scaffolding to develop their comprehension skills.

Strategies for Building Connections

Students who have not had meaningful encounters with the experiences and situations presented in books chosen for read-alouds may have difficulty comprehending such texts. This is also true when students have limited knowledge of language structure and text structure. The following evidence-based strategies will facilitate the processes of building ELLs' conceptual knowledge and finding and strengthening connections between their experiences and the themes presented in read-aloud texts:

- Use simple oral language to *describe critical attributes* or main elements of the theme prior to reading the text aloud and refer to such attributes as necessary when discussing the text.

- *Focus on important elements and details* of the title and illustrations within the book while conducting a picture walk through the book prior to reading it aloud.

- When appropriate, *use synonymous terms* in the students' first language to clarify confusing terms in the second language. Or, in cases where instruction is delivered exclusively in only one language, scaffold instruction by using terms that are at the students' level of comprehensible input or language proficiency. For example, if a text talks about a child who fidgets a lot, a teacher conducting the read-aloud with ELLs in English might clarify this term by using simpler language with which the students are familiar. In this case the teacher might explain that *fidgets* means that the child moves her body a lot—even when sitting—or plays with little toys or things when she is supposed to be paying attention. A teacher who is bilingual in Spanish, reading an English book aloud to students whose first language is Spanish, might clarify the term *fidgets* by explaining, *el niño está muy inquieto* [the child is restless].

- *Draw parallels* between students' general knowledge that is culture- or experience-specific and material in the text as a way of clarifying the reality of diverse contexts and cultures. For example, if a story describes a child shopping with his family at an outdoor food market, similarities can be drawn to students' own experiences shopping with their families at the grocery store or at an outdoor flea market.

- In addition to explicitly teaching target vocabulary words, *clarify other terms that may be important for understanding* main concepts presented in the text.

- *Make text-to-text connections* so that students use newly acquired knowledge to understand new text. For example, if a previously studied vocabulary word appears in a subsequent read-aloud text, call students' attention to the word and discuss its meaning in the new text. Or if a new text presents information related to a topic covered in a previous one, point that out, connecting the information to broaden students' knowledge and strengthen their understanding of informational relationships.

One particular activity that is an integral part of the read-aloud experience is for the teacher to introduce the book on the first day of reading by displaying its cover, reading the title and the names of the author and illustrator, and examining the book's illustrations. As noted above, this kind of preview, or picture walk through the book, is a particularly important step for ELLs with respect to soliciting and activating their prior knowledge and language with respect to the book's content. It also gives teachers opportunities to help students build other comprehension skills, such as predicting what the book will be about or making connections with other texts they have heard or read that have similar themes.

Research to Practice: Reflecting on Teaching and Learning

1. Consider the different ways you group students for varied instructional purposes. What are some of the positive outcomes of working with small groups? What are some of the challenges? How might you think of structuring small-group read-aloud sessions in ways that maximize learning and language use for ELLs in your classroom, according to the strategies presented in this chapter?

2. Reflect on some of the background experiences and interests of the students in your class. What types of texts might you choose that would tap into their interests and cultural and life experiences?

3. Select a book that you might typically use for read-aloud purposes. Analyze the text for sentence length, complexity of ideas, and cultural and experiential meaning. In thinking about your students' language proficiency levels and experiences as well as the concepts described in this chapter, do you think this is an appropriate book to read aloud? Why or why not?

4. How might you incorporate strategic read-alouds into content areas other than language arts?

Suggested Readings for Further Study

Hirsch, E.D., Willingham, D.T., & Neuman, S.B. (2006). Background knowledge: The case for content-rich curriculum core for the early grades. *American Educator, Spring.*

Hirsch, E.D. (2006). Building knowledge: The case for bringing content into the language arts block and for a knowledge-rich curriculum core for all children. *American Educator, 30*(1), 8–17.

Spangenberg-Urbschat, K., & Pritchard, R. (1994). *Kids come in all languages: Reading instruction for ESL students.* Newark, DE: International Reading Association.

CHAPTER 3

Active Engagement With Vocabulary

Mrs. Salinas: (third-grade ESL teacher) Yesterday we learned the words miserable, enter, and comfortable. What does the word miserable mean?

Isabel: (an ELL student) Feel bad. I feel miserable sick.

Mrs. Salinas: Yes, we learned that miserable means to feel in a very sad and lonely way—it means to feel bad. And I also feel miserable when I am sick. Everyone, let's say that together. "I feel miserable when I am sick."

Mrs. Salinas works throughout the day in general education classrooms with small groups of students during their 90-minute language arts blocks. As a third-grade teacher working in an urban district, she realizes that the literacy demands placed on her students are greater than they were in the primary grades. Now that they are at the intermediate level, the stakes are higher; it is urgent that her students acquire strong academic English vocabulary and language skills as soon as possible. Without these skills, her students will only fall further and further behind.

Mrs. Salinas knows what she's doing. Vocabulary knowledge is a vital element of listening and reading comprehension (National Institute of Child Health and Human Development [NICHD], 2000). And for young children who may not yet be reading or reading fluently, listening to stories and other kinds of text read aloud provides valuable opportunities for them to learn new vocabulary, including vocabulary associated with academic language and higher order, complex thought.

In fact, in the words of Stahl and Stahl (2004),

Storybook reading is the most powerful source of new vocabulary, including those academic words that are valued in school discourse. Books are literally "where the words are... ." The average difficulty of a typical children's book ranks above that of either a children's or an adult television program and above that of a typical conversation between two college-educated adults.... Even a book like *Curious George Takes a Job* (Rey, 1947), intended for first graders to read and younger children to listen to, contains relatively rare words, not only *curious* but also *cozy, dizzy, wound, scold, attention*—just from the first 20 pages. (p. 67)

Teachers can capitalize on this opportunity to build language with their students through strategic read-aloud sessions characterized by dynamic instruction in vocabulary knowledge and use.

ELLs and Vocabulary

Research has shown that ELLs often "know fewer English vocabulary words than monolingual English speakers but, in addition, know less about the meaning of those words" (August, Carlo, Dressler, & Snow, 2005, p. 51; Verhallen & Schoonen, 1993). Yet it is precisely this breadth and depth of word knowledge that is vital to comprehension, especially for ELLs (August et al., 2005). Due to their limited English-language proficiency, they also have more difficulty inferring meaning from context (Carlo et al., 2004).

Researchers have found that students who are already somewhat literate in their first language have an advantage when it comes to learning a second language (see Chapter 1). Specifically, they can "take advantage of higher order vocabulary skills in the first language, such as the ability to provide formal definitions and interpret metaphors, when speaking a second language" (August & Shanahan, 2006; Executive Summary, p. 5).

Instruction designed to build language and word knowledge, then, must further ELLs' understanding of word meanings, shades of meaning, and their uses across contexts, as well as the relationships between words (e.g., members of the same word family, synonyms, antonyms, homographs, homonyms).

Strategies That Help ELLs Learn Vocabulary

Summarizing studies related to vocabulary instruction across the elementary grades, the report of the National Reading Panel (NICHD, 2000) concludes the following:

- Vocabulary should be taught both explicitly and implicitly to have the most impact on acquisition. It is particularly important to use explicit instruction for vocabulary from texts students hear read aloud or read independently, both to ensure comprehension and to increase the likelihood that the vocabulary will be incorporated into their daily language. Carlo et al. (2004) also finds direct vocabulary instruction particularly helpful for ELLs in bilingual and English-dominant classrooms.

- Although there is a small likelihood that students' vocabulary will increase simply through exposure to words they hear read aloud—a concept known as *incidental exposure*—teachers should nevertheless take advantage of opportunities to explicitly teach ELLs how specific strategies can help them deduce word meanings (e.g., using context clues; Carlo et al., 2004).

- Active participation on the part of students in student-initiated speech, participation in discussions about vocabulary, and repetition of the meanings of words is important to learning; asking and answering questions during the read-aloud results in more learning than just listening to the story (Teale, 2003).

- Active engagement on the part of students in activities that promote use of words in original sentences significantly influences students' vocabulary acquisition and comprehension outcomes (Carlo et al., 2004).

- Specific and explicit teaching of vocabulary words, especially in the context of meaningful and interesting stories and other texts, has been shown to increase students' memory, understanding, and correct use of those words (Vaughn-Shavuo, 1990).

- Repeated read-alouds of a story produce higher gains in vocabulary than single readings. Also, the more often a particular word is used during a story read-aloud, the more the likely it is that students will remember its meaning (Morrow & Brittain, 2003).

- Multiple and repeated exposures to words in different contexts is critical to vocabulary development for ELLs (Carlo et al., 2004).

- Preteaching vocabulary words from the text prior to reading it aloud positively influences vocabulary acquisition and comprehension.

Specific and focused instruction in vocabulary is also critical for ELLs in that it builds content-related schema (knowledge) and oral language proficiency (NICHD, 2000). By explicitly teaching the meanings and uses of words in and across contexts teachers help students (a) understand how language is used in different contexts and (b) access important concept and background knowledge that increases comprehension. Explicit instruction along with multiple exposures to words also helps ELLs build academic language proficiency that in turn contributes to increased literacy.

Planning the Vocabulary Portion of the Read-Aloud Experience

So how does one use all of this information to create effective vocabulary lessons? And what does an effective vocabulary lesson look like, especially in the context of strategic read-alouds with ELLs?

One way to infuse the read-aloud experience with effective vocabulary instruction is to efficiently and effectively plan read-aloud sessions to reflect the best-practice elements discussed in Chapter 2. Figure 4 depicts the sequence of steps involved in this process.

The process begins with the teacher selecting an appropriate text and then reviewing the entire book to identify critical knowledge (e.g., main idea and characters in a storybook or new information about a topic in an informational text) as well as any concepts that might be difficult for students to understand. This knowledge will become the focus of activities the teacher will use to preview the book with students and to build their background knowledge prior to reading the book aloud.

For example, because the main ideas in the storybook *The Great Kapok Tree* (Cherry, 2000; also available in Spanish) focus on conservation of the rainforest, it would be important for a teacher to plan on activating students' prior knowledge about both the concept of conservation as well as the rainforest before reading this book aloud. It is also important for the teacher to note that the main character in the book falls asleep and has a dream in which animals appear and speak to him; this part of the book may be confusing for some

Figure 4. Vocabulary Instruction Sequence for Strategic Read-Aloud Lessons

1. Select meaningful texts at appropriate levels of language proficiency.

2. Preview text for main ideas, concepts, vocabulary used throughout, and contextual use of vocabulary.

| 2a. Divide text into approximately five, 200–250 word passages. | 2b. Choose 3–4 vocabulary words per passage, and creates a meaning for each word. | 2c. Using index cards, write each word on one side of a card and its meaning on the other side. |

students (e.g., those with lower levels of language proficiency) if it is not made clear through explicit discussion that the character is having a dream. In such a discussion, the teacher could also talk with students about their own dreams, asking them if they ever had a dream that seemed so realistic they were not sure if they really had been dreaming.

Next the teacher rereads the book, looking for natural breaks in the text every 200–250 words or so, and divides the text into separate sections at those breaks. Plans are made to read one section of the book aloud each day over a period of three to five days, depending on the book's length. Since the goal is to target vocabulary and listening comprehension skills, the teacher chooses three to four words from each section to focus on and creates a meaning for each. How to choose and define these words is discussed next, followed by thoughts on how to teach them through the read-aloud activities.

Selecting Vocabulary Words to Teach

The frequency and utility of new vocabulary are the most important factors teachers need to consider when choosing words to teach (NICHD, 2000). Particularly for ELLs, comprehending common high-frequency words (those that appear most often in texts, such as *what, said, in, is, it, people, many, through*) and high-utility words (those deemed most useful for navigating one's environment, such as *next, often, important, most, about, where, not, do, want, have, here, there, around*) is critical, especially for those with lower levels of language proficiency.

What's more, teachers should consider teaching high-frequency and high-utility words encountered across content areas, as knowledge of such words contributes to increased academic language proficiency. For example, *together* is a word that students would benefit from learning because it is used with high frequency in language arts and across other content areas. The word *polygon*, however, is not used often in speech or text. It is highly content-specific and typically used only in math or science lessons. Teaching this word would be important, though, if text comprehension is dependent on knowing the word or understanding the concept it represents.

Descriptive words (adjectives and adverbs) and action words (verbs), which are often easier to learn than nouns, are also valuable words to target for explicit instruction. Important as well are words that can be demonstrated or visualized; words that have similar meanings and uses in the students' first language; and cognates, words that are similar in spelling and meaning across languages (Beck, McKeown, & Kucan, 2002; NICHD, 2000).

A Special Note on Cognates

Explicitly teaching cognates to ELLs is particularly useful in building their language skills, vocabulary, and comprehension. Research has shown that, depending on the first language of students, highlighting cognates across students' first and second languages can greatly improve their vocabulary acquisition and comprehension (August & Shanahan, 2006; Calderón et al., 2005; Nagy, García, Durgunoglu, & Hancin-Bhatt, 1993).

Many of the Romance languages, or languages with Latin roots, include words with similar spellings and meanings. Examples of English–Spanish cognates include *family–familia, insect–insecto, decision–decisión*. As students progress in their schooling and content area courses, they will encounter many more words with Latin roots and, thus, many more cognates. This is especially true in the sciences. However, it is also true that even young children, if their first language has Latin roots, encounter cognates on an almost daily basis. Calling students' attention to the similarities between cognates can significantly increase ELLs' vocabulary acquisition and comprehension skills. Explicit instruction in recognizing cognates and their identification will highlight their usefulness (August, Calderón, & Carlo, 2002; Nagy et al., 1993).

The issue of teaching cognates is further complicated by the fact that some cognates (e.g., *paternal–paterno, decisive–decisivo*) are considered higher-level words and, as such, require more linguistic sophistication to understand. As a result, despite being cognates, such words might not be the best choices for explicit instruction. For example, the word *difícil* in Spanish is the commonly used word for *difficult* or *hard* in English. However, the word *difficult* is generally considered a high-level vocabulary word in English; children in the primary grades are more apt to use the more basic word *hard* to describe a task. Similarly, in Spanish, the word *legumbres* (*legumes* in English) is a very common word meaning *vegetables*. However, in English the word *legumes* is a more scientific or technical term and not often used in everyday life.

Also problematic are "false cognates," words that look the same but mean very different things. English–Spanish false cognates include such words as *rope–ropa* (in Spanish, *clothing*), *soap–sopa* (in Spanish, *soup*), and *large–largo* (in Spanish, *long*).

Figure 5 summarizes the types of words teachers should consider teaching during the vocabulary portion of read-aloud sessions.

Levels of Word Difficulty

Beck and colleagues (2002) identify three tiers of words, differentiated by their level of academic use and utility, to guide the selection of vocabulary words

Figure 5. Types of Words to Target for Vocabulary Instruction for ELLs

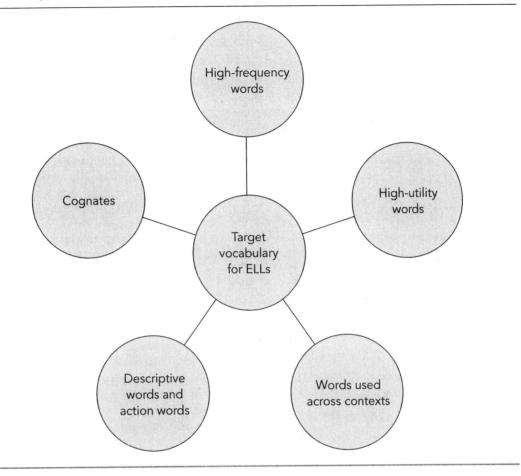

to teach. Calderón et al. (2005) modifies Beck, McKeown, and Kucan's tiers to meet the needs of students who are transitioning from Spanish to English reading (see Table 3).

Calderón et al. contend that, for ELLs, a word's level of difficulty depends both on the context in which it is used and their own language proficiency levels in both their first and second languages. It then follows that to choose appropriate words to teach—words at a student's level of comprehensible input—a teacher must be very familiar with their students' language proficiency levels.

Calderón et al.'s criteria for selecting vocabulary from texts to use in explicit instruction takes into account (a) whether the word is concrete or can easily be explained or demonstrated; (b) if it is a cognate, and if so, what level of cognate; (c) the ways in which a word can be used differently or meaningfully

Table 3. Suggested Tiers of Vocabulary Difficulty for ELLs

Word level	General descriptors (Beck et al., 2002)	General descriptors adapted for ELLs (Calderón et al., 2005)
Tier I words	Words that for students with basic language proficiency do not usually require explicit instruction (e.g., *sad, run, table, food, eat, red, blue, butterfly, dog*)	Basic words and high-frequency cognates (e.g., *family–familia*) for which students have understanding in their first language but may not know in English; also high-frequency false cognates (e.g., *pan*, in Spanish, meaning *bread*, not *pan* in English); and simple idiomatic expressions or common phrases (e.g., *let's move on, hop in the car, it's a piece of cake*) that can be taught easily through visuals, demonstrations, or simple explanations
Tier II words	High-utility words that are more engaging, more academic in nature, or more precise descriptors of Tier I words (e.g., *nimble, portion, humungous, groceries, devour, gold*)	High-frequency and high-utility words used in student texts across content areas as described by Beck, McKeown and Kucan (2002); also high-frequency, multiple-meaning words (e.g., *ring, play, time*) that require explicit instruction or demonstration; and cognates that are high-frequency in Spanish but not in English (e.g., *demonstration–demonstración, frequent–frecuencia, opportunity–oportunidad*)
Tier III words	Words that are highly specific or technical; usually relegated to specific fields, content areas, or processes; or used with very low frequency (e.g., *photosynthesis, proton, molting, everglades*)	Words that are highly specific or technical, as described by Beck and colleagues (2002), with which ELL students are unfamiliar and therefore must be taught explicitly and in context; also cognates with dissimilar spellings (e.g., *tend–atender, maintain–mantener*)

across contexts; and (d) the word's utility value, or the extent to which it is useful to students.

Tier I Words

Tier I words are basic words (or equivalent cognates), representing ideas, concepts, or objects with which most students have familiarity. As a result, students do not typically need explicit instruction in these words. Examples include *happy, sit, chair, jump, small,* and *red,* as well as English–Spanish cognates such as *problem–problema, cafeteria–cafetería, banana–banana, animal–animal,* and *cereal–cereal.* When explicit instruction of Tier I words is necessary, teachers can demonstrate or provide concrete examples of the words or point out parallel words in the student's first language as a way of clarifying meaning.

Tier II Words

Tier II words are high-utility words that are more engaging, more academic in nature, or more precise descriptors than Tier I words. Calderón et al. (2005, p. 124) describe Tier II words for ELLs as those that

- "Have importance and utility (i.e., they are characteristic of mature language users and appear frequently across a variety of domains)"
- "Have instructional potential (i.e., they can be worked with in a variety of ways so that students can build rich representations of them and their connections to other words and concepts)"
- "Provide precision and specificity in describing ideas for which students already have a basic conceptual understanding"

Tier II words occur frequently in the text of children's books, yet they are not as familiar to students as Tier I words. As a result, some of these words will need to be explicitly taught, depending on students' prior language and experiential backgrounds.

In Latin-based languages, Tier II words also include higher-level cognates, such as *opportunity–oportunidad* that might be high-frequency words in a student's first language but low-frequency words in English. For example, a Tier II word such as *scamper* could be defined for a student by using the Tier I word *run* and then adding the phrase *in a happy and fun way* to give *scamper* more contextual meaning. Similarly, the teacher might define the word *groceries* by using the Tier I word *food,* already understood by the students, and then adding the phrase *that you buy at a store.*

When teachers use terms with which students are already acquainted to give meaning to new words, students are better able to associate the new vocabulary with their daily experiences, making them more likely to generalize its use across contexts. In this way, students gain greater sophistication and depth in their ability to describe familiar situations and use language in meaningful, interesting, and important ways (Beck et al., 2002).

Tier II words are encountered often in text and can be academic in nature. Typically, however, they are engaging and descriptive, offering students new ways to state already understood concepts. These words, according to Gersten and Baker (2000), are the types of words that are critical to the development of ELLs' language flexibility and ability to elaborate on a subject. Again, teachers need to pay attention to students' language proficiency levels to determine if and when they need explicit instruction in Tier II words.

Tier III Words

Tier III words are words that are technical in nature and specific to a particular content area or process. They occur very infrequently in narrative texts and are more common in informational books; as such, they need to be taught explicitly when they are needed to ensure understanding in a given context. For students who are monolingual English speakers, these words are usually learned incidentally through contextual use; however, most ELLs will require explicit instruction in these words. Examples of Tier III words include technical terms associated with math or science concepts (e.g., *polygon, condensation)* and cognates with dissimilar spellings (e.g., *marvelous–maravilloso, battle–batalla)*.

Selecting Words for Explicit Instruction

Given the sheer number of words within any given text with which students may be unfamiliar, teachers need to consider the language levels, experiences, interests, and developmental levels of their students when deciding which words to target for explicit instruction. Reflecting on the two following questions may help teachers determine if a particular word should be chosen:

1. Can the word or the knowledge the word conveys *be linked to* other words or concepts students already know and, as a result, make them *better able to* describe their own life experiences?
2. Will learning the word *facilitate a deeper understanding* of a specific context within a story that can also be linked to the student's own knowledge or life experiences (Beck et al., 2002)?

For example, many young children are both fascinated by and anxious during thunderstorms. The book *Thundercake* by Patricia Polacco (1990) vividly describes a young girl's experience baking a thundercake with her grandmother as a thunderstorm draws closer and closer. The child's anxiety is mediated by the loving relationship she has with her grandmother and the fun activity they experience together. One word out of many that might be appropriate to teach students as part of a read-aloud of this book is the verb *scurried* (as in "'Now let's gather all the things we'll need!' she exclaimed as she *scurried* toward the back door," p. 5). *Scurried* would be a fitting vocabulary word to teach ELLs because of the following reasons:

- The general meaning of the word (having to hurry in an organized way to get something done quickly before time runs out) is familiar to many students.
- The word is a verb or action word and is easy to visualize.
- The word is a high-frequency word that students will encounter across multiple contexts such as during play, in conversation, and in language arts texts.
- The word is a high-utility word that will be useful in everyday conversation.
- Students will be able to relate the context in which the word is used in the story to similar events or moments in their own daily lives.

Again, teachers should choose words that will increase students' language proficiency levels—a process that must take into account contextual elements that may be unique to a particular classroom or group of students. For example, in cases where students have limited prior exposure to specific words and concepts, teachers may need to provide them with explicit instruction, not only in Tier III words but also in Tier I and Tier II words.

In general, teachers should teach three to four words from each section of the text selected for a read-aloud lesson; at that rate, students will experience vocabulary growth but will not be overwhelmed by unrealistic memory demands.

Defining Words Selected for Explicit Instruction

General Guidelines

Often the idea of vocabulary development carries with it a sense of having to learn technical-sounding definitions that are sometimes hard to comprehend and lack contextual understanding. For example, the dictionary definition of the word *delicious* is "very pleasing, delightful; highly pleasing to the senses" (Merriam-Webster Online Kids Dictionary). Clearly, this is not a definition using simple language that primary-grade children would typically use or understand.

For the purposes of building language, a more student-centered way of "defining" words is to provide students with word meanings that capture the way words are used in context or relate to students' backgrounds. In creating such meanings, teachers should try to think of similar words or phrases that the students might use to describe a particular word within the context it is used in the story (Beck et al., 2002). When such an approach is used, students are more apt to fully understand and remember the meaning of the word and how it was used. For example, instead of giving students the dictionary definition of the word *delicious*, teachers might instead provide them with a meaning that uses a phrase the students might use, such as *tastes very good*.

Obviously, to create effective meanings for words, teachers must take into account what they know about students' levels of first- and second-language proficiency. Meanings should be contextually accurate yet, at the same time, comprehensible to the students.

For example, if a teacher chooses to teach the word *sample*, the meaning provided to the students should correspond with the way it is used in the text: either as a verb (to *sample* the cookies) or as a noun (to made a *sample* so they could see how to do it). If at another point in time the students encounter the word in a different context, both meanings can be discussed. Of course, if the students are already familiar with the alternate meaning of the word or bring up the dual meanings when the word is defined, an immediate discussion of both meanings would be appropriate.

Beck and colleagues (2002) suggest that when teachers create a meaning for a word they try to capture the essence of its definition rather than focus on a specific aspect of its definition, which might in fact be misleading or difficult to understand. In their book *Bringing Words to Life: Robust Vocabulary Instruction*, two definitions are contrasted for the word *meticulous*. When the word is defined as *extremely careful about small details*, students can very easily focus on the word *careful*—often used in the sense of watching out for danger—and as a result use *meticulous* in the wrong context. However, the definition *being careful and neat about small details* provides a clearer understanding of what the word really means. In another context, the teacher might explain that *amble* means *to walk slowly and easily* as opposed to *to walk slowly and leisurely*, as the word *easily* is more apt to be understood by young children than is the word *leisurely*.

Defining Words That Are Difficult to Visualize

When teaching ELLs, it is also critical to teach students the meanings and uses of high-frequency, functional words that are abstract and hard to visualize, including articles, prepositions, auxiliary verbs, conjunctions, and other indeterminate "pointing words" such as *the, a, can, may, which, that, do, not, could, would*, and *does*. ELLs often have difficulty with these types of words because they may not be present or are used in different speech patterns in their first language.

Articles, prepositions, and "function words" (Minskoff, 2005) can be explicitly taught, however, by

- Comparing them—if students' first-language proficiency levels make such comparisons feasible—to similar words or ideas that exist in the first language
- Giving examples—across different contexts—of how such words are used in sentences; explicitly pointing out where they fit in sentences; and noting as well their inappropriate use (e.g., using the article *a* to precede a plural noun)
- By having students "act out" the meaning of the word, as in the case of some prepositions and directional words

Consider the following two sentences, which a teacher might use to teach students the meaning of the word *could*:

They asked if they *could* ride their bikes to the park.

Their mother said that they *could.*

The teacher might begin by providing a meaning such as *were allowed to*, or *had permission.* In a bilingual English–Spanish context, the teacher might further clarify the meaning of *could* by referencing the Spanish words *permitir* or *permiso* and by saying, "Ellos pidieron permiso de montar sus bicicletas al parque. La mamá les dió permiso/les permitió." Again, contextual use of the word is critical. For example, another meaning of *could*, in a different context, might be *to be able to* in a physical sense (e.g., She could reach it.). It is important to remember that the key to vocabulary instruction for ELLs is explicit discussion of how and when words are used, multiple exposure to words across contexts, and use of their first language when possible to clarify meanings.

Table 4 summarizes the guidelines for creating meanings for vocabulary words targeted for explicit instruction during strategic read-aloud sessions.

Application in the Classroom

The way in which the concepts discussed above can be applied to strategic read-aloud sessions for first graders is graphically illustrated in two different ways. First, Table 5 focuses on the popular picture book *A House for Hermit Crab*

Table 4. Creating Meanings for Targeted Vocabulary Words

- Use dictionary definitions as a reference only, if at all
- Use words or phrases students themselves might use
- Use low-tier words with which students are already familiar to provide meanings for high-tier words
- Provide meaning for the word as it is used in the context of the story; teachers may expand on the word's use in other contexts later, if appropriate
- Provide meanings that reflect the essence of, rather than just a part of, a word's definition
- Define low-tier words using contextual clues, or if possible, refer to the word in the students' first language

by Eric Carle, a text chosen for use during a strategic read-aloud. This book is written by an author who is familiar to many primary-grade teachers and revolves around themes that may draw on the experiences of students, such as feeling vulnerable, making new friends, and growing up and experiencing new places and adventures. Although the text is a work of fiction and not considered informational per se, the book teaches young children something about different types of sea creatures. It is also structured in such a way that the crab's adventures follow a predictable, monthly sequence.

In Table 5, the first 250 words of the book are reproduced, and sample vocabulary words a teacher might target for explicit instruction during a strategic read-aloud session are highlighted in boldface type. The second column of the table provides the rationale for choosing those particular words in light of the previous discussion of what types of words might be appropriate for students. Of course, words an individual teacher chooses must align with his or her own students' levels of language proficiency and language development, and only three to four words from each 250-word passage would ultimately be chosen. Note that the difficult-to-visualize word *but* is one of the words a teacher might select.

This example highlights a variety of words a teacher might choose to target for explicit instruction during a strategic read-aloud session along with various reasons for those choices. Yet it is possible that equally valid reasons could be provided for choosing different words. The ultimate choice depends on students' language proficiency levels and background knowledge. What is critical is for teachers to choose words that allow students to describe familiar concepts with higher-level vocabulary. Also, students should be taught words that will deepen their understanding of the context of the story that is read aloud with respect to their own life experiences (Beck et al., 2002). In doing so, teachers of ELLs provide their students with rich, meaningful, engaging

Table 5. Targeted Vocabulary Words From *A House for Hermit Crab*

The opening 250-word passage of *A House for Hermit Crab* with vocabulary targeted for explicit instruction highlighted	Type of vocabulary word targeted and rationale for selection
"Time to **move**," said Hermit Crab one day in January. "I've grown too big for this little shell."	**move**: Verb. A good Tier I word for students with lower proficiency. Could be considered higher-level because of its dual meanings (to move one's home vs. to move one's body). (Spanish equivalent: mudarse vs. moverse)
He had felt safe and **snug** in his shell. But now it was too **snug**. Hermit Crab stepped out of the shell and onto the floor of the ocean.	**snug**: Adjective. Tier II word for tight or a close fit. Easily visualized, high utility.
But it was **frightening** out in the open sea without a shell to hide in. "What if a big fish comes along and **attacks** me?" he thought. "I must find a new house soon."	**But**: Signal/function word. Hard to visualize, high frequency, high utility. (Spanish equivalent: pero) **frightening**: Adverb. Tier II word for scary. Easily visualized, high utility. **attacks**: Verb. Tier II word for fight. Easily visualized, high utility. (Cognate to Spanish atacar)
Early in February, Hermit Crab found just the house he was looking for. It was a big shell, and strong. He moved right in **wiggling** and waggling about inside it to see how it felt. It felt just right. "But it looks so—well, so *plain*," thought Hermit Crab.	**wiggling**: Verb. Tier II word for moving side to side. Easily visualized, high utility. **plain**: Adjective. Tier II for simple. High frequency, high utility. Used multiple times in the book and across other texts and multiple content areas.
In March, Hermit Crab met some sea anemones. They **swayed** gently back and forth in the water.	**swayed**: Verb. Tier II for moving back and forth, the meaning given in the text. Easily visualized, high utility.
"How **beautiful** you are!" said Hermit Crab. "Would one of you be willing to come and live on my house? It is so **plain**, it needs you." "I'll come," whispered a small sea anemone. Gently, Hermit Crab picked it up with his claw and put it on his shell.	**beautiful**: Adjective. Tier II for pretty. High utility, multiple occurrences across contexts and texts. **plain**: see above.
In April, Hermit Crab passed a **flock** of starfish moving **slowly** along the sea floor.	**flock**: Noun. Tier II for a group of creatures or animals. Easily visualized. Multiple uses across content areas. **slowly**: Adverb. A terrific Tier I word for students at lower levels of English proficiency.
"How **handsome** you are!" said Hermit Crab.	**handsome**: Adjective. Tier 1, as students typically have a word with the same meaning in their first language. High utility.
"Would one of you be willing to **decorate** my house?" "I would," **signaled** a little sea star.	**decorate**: Verb. Tier II for to cover with things you like. Easily visualized, high utility. Cognate to Spanish decorar **signal (signaled)**: Verb. Tier II for to wave, to show you want something. High utility, multiple uses across contexts.
Carefully, Hermit Crab picked it up with his claw and put it on his house.	

Note. From Carle, E. (1991). *A house for hermit crab.* New York: Simon and Schuster. Reprinted with permission.

opportunities to increase their language proficiency (Anderson & Roit, 1998; Gersten & Baker, 2000).

Table 6 provides a second example of how the principles of vocabulary selection and definition discussed above can be used by classroom teachers. In this case, the vocabulary words presented were taken from a number of different books written in English and Spanish. Including books in both languages is intended to help guide the work of ELL teachers working in different types of programs (e.g., monolingual, ESL with language support, bilingual). Also presented are the meanings created for each of the targeted words.

Again, it is important to keep in mind that two teachers reading the exact same book aloud to their classes may target completely different words, depending on the language proficiency levels and experiential backgrounds of their respective students. Furthermore, word selection is guided by each teacher's perception of the usefulness of individual words across contexts. Nevertheless, the ultimate goal of all teachers selecting and defining words to target for direction instruction during strategic read alouds remains the same: to increase students' overall levels of language proficiency by increasing their understanding of words that are content based and of high utility, frequency, and interest.

Strategies for Generalizing Word Knowledge

As stated at the beginning of this chapter, engaging students in discussions of vocabulary meanings and activities that require them to use words in structured ways helps promote vocabulary acquisition (Carlo et al., 2004; Morrow & Brittain, 2003; Vaughn-Shavuo, 1990). We now turn our attention to specific strategies within the read-aloud procedure that give students opportunities to learn new vocabulary words and then use those words appropriately in social and academic situations. One way to provide these types of opportunities is to structure the vocabulary portion of the read-aloud experience in three segments: (1) preteaching vocabulary prior to reading the passage; (2) highlighting when and in what context the vocabulary is heard in the passage; and (3) engaging students in quick, meaningful activities that provide concrete examples and nonexamples of the use of the target words (Minskoff, 2005; Vacca et al., 2003).

Preteaching Vocabulary

After choosing a text for the read-aloud, selecting appropriate words from the text to teach, and creating meanings for those words, teachers begin the

Table 6. Targeted English and Spanish Vocabulary Words From Selected Texts

Theme/text selected	Sample words/meanings
Theme: Families Book: *A Chair For My Mother* (Williams, 1984)	**silverware** *(n)*, forks, spoons and knives **speech** *(n)*, a talk someone gives about something **boost** *(v)*, lift or push up **wrap** *(v)*, cover or put something (cloth, paper, plastic) all around something else **delivered** *(v)*, brought
Theme: Pets Book: *Dogs* (Gibbons, 1997)	**bares** *(v)*, shows **restless** *(adj)*, moving around a lot **social** *(adj)*, friendly, knowing how to get along with others **confined** *(adj)*, covered or closed in, not open **secure** *(adj)*, safe **unattended** *(adj)*, alone, no one else nearby or watching **guard** *(v)*, protect **miniature** *(adj)*, a very small thing
Theme: Insects Book: *Ant Cities* (Dorros, 1998)	**grooming** *(v)*, cleaning **capture** *(v)*, grab or take to keep **devour** *(v)*, eat up quickly and completely **hollowed-out** [hollow] *(adj)*, open on the inside **pavement** *(n)*, sidewalk or roadway
Theme: Serpientes (Snakes) Book: *Las serpientes y nosotros* (*Snakes and Us*; Stone, 1991)	**enfrenten** (enfrentar) *(v)*, tienen **subsistir** *(v)*, vivir **hábitat** *(n)*, el lugar donde vive **desinfectar** *(v)*, limpiar muy bien para quitar gérmenes o veneno **mortal** *(adj)*, que puede causar el muerte **adecuada** *(adj)*, buena, apta, hábil
Theme: Cuidar a la Tierra (Caring for the Earth) Book: *Sara vio una guacamaya azúl* (*Sara Saw a Blue Macaw*; Bogart & Daigneault, 1991)	**sacudió** (sacudir) *(v)*, movió de lado a lado rápidamente **orilla** *(n)*, el lado del río, dónde se encuentra la tierra **aletear** *(v)*, mover las alas **descubrió** (descubrir) *(v)*, observó, encontró **pose** *(n)*, postura, un puesto del cuerpo **ingeniosa** *(adj)*, lista, inteligente
Theme: Animales del Mar (Sea Animals) Book: *Nutrias de Mar* (*Sea Otters*; Palmer, 1991)	**criaturas** *(n)*, seres, animales **promedio** *(n)*, tamaño **traseros** *(adj)*, los de atrás **flojamente** *(adv)*, muy relajada, fácilmente **condiciones** *(n)*, estados de ser **probablemente** *(adv)*, casi seguro o cierto, pero no completamente

instructional portion of the read-aloud session. First, teachers briefly introduce each word and provide the meaning for the word. Students should repeat the word and its meaning after the teacher. The word can be written on an index card with the meaning on the back of the card or on sentence strips, a white board, or chart paper—anything that will serve as a reference. This is appropriate even if students are not yet reading connected text.

The teacher then gives students a few examples of each word in a sentence, maintaining the same meaning of the word that was provided to the students. Students might also be encouraged to think of times they have heard the word being used or to give an example themselves. This portion of the activity should remain brief, with all the words introduced within three to five minutes. It is important to get to the actual read-aloud, at which point students actually hear the words in the context of the story in a timely manner.

If students do not have the background needed to understand the selected vocabulary words, teachers may need to spend a few days talking about the topic with the students before reading the book aloud. The goal of these discussions would be to increase students' background knowledge and experiential language as it relates to the topic. It is important to remember, however, that read-aloud texts and vocabulary should align with and build students' schema and language; if too much preteaching is necessary, it may mean that the text is inappropriate for use in a read-aloud lesson.

Listen for the Words in the Text

After introducing the target words and their meanings to students, the teacher reads through the passage once in its entirety. Following this initial reading, which generally takes from five to eight minutes, teachers should spend a few minutes focusing on comprehension through guided discussion of the main elements of the passage. Ways in which to plan for and execute comprehension activities will be discussed in detail in Chapter 5.

At this point, the passage is read once more. During this second reading, students listen for the target words, and when each is discovered, the reading is temporarily stopped so that students can discuss the word in context and participate in quick activities. These activities could include asking students to listen to the teacher model the use of the word and then use the word themselves to complete a sentence stem, known as a framed sentence (a sentence in which part of the sentence is left out for students to fill in with their own ideas). Alternatively, students could act out characteristics of the word. Teachers informally assess students' understanding of the word during these activities. The teacher then resumes reading the passage until the next vocabulary word is encountered, which prompts another short round of activities related to use of that word in context. This pattern continues until all words are discussed.

Figure 6 provides an example of the types and sequence of vocabulary activities a teacher might use during a read-aloud session. These activities would be incorporated into the second reading of the text.

By engaging in this quick sequence of activities, students receive multiple exposures to each vocabulary word, its meaning, and its contextual use. They are also actively involved in student-initiated talk, repetition of word meanings, and discussion about vocabulary (NICHD, 2000; Wasik & Bond, 2001).

Teachers should keep in mind that they may need to scaffold vocabulary instruction for students with lower levels of oral language proficiency. Such students, for example, may need a teacher to help them structure their responses by providing them with sentence stems.

As students advance in their language proficiency, activities such as those previously described are valuable in that they give students opportunities to use new vocabulary in many ways, including the construction of original sentences. Such opportunities serve to further increase students' language flexibility and elaboration skills.

The read-aloud concludes with the teacher briefly summarizing and discussing the segment of the text read that day and encouraging students to listen for and use the new vocabulary words they just learned throughout the day, if possible. This portion of the read-aloud generally takes from 10–12 minutes.

The next day, the teacher begins the read-aloud session with a cumulative review of the previous day's vocabulary words and then introduces and discusses four to five new words found in the second segment of the book. The teacher follows the same procedure as the day before, reading the segment aloud in its entirety once, and then incorporating vocabulary-building activities into a second reading of the segment. In this way, the entire text is read aloud in segments over three to five consecutive days.

On the day after reading the last 250-word segment of text, the teacher reviews the book with the students. Specifically, the teacher asks the students to retell the story using the new vocabulary they have learned as they take a teacher-led picture walk through the entire book. Teachers can also use this day to review four to five of the most challenging vocabulary in the text through activities such as having students act out the words, composing a class story using the words, or using the words to play charades or matching games. The goal of instruction on this day is to give students additional instruction in comprehension and to engage in practice with word use.

Figure 6. Strategic Read-Aloud Vocabulary Activities

Text: *Chrysanthemum* (Henkes, 1996, pp. 22–30)

Vocabulary words:
humorous *(adj)*, funny
beam [beamed] *(v)*, to be happy in a way that your whole body seems alive
longingly *(adv)*, in a way that shows you want something a lot

The teacher preteaches the vocabulary words, saying them out loud, explaining their meanings, and asking the students to repeat them. Then the teacher gives an example of each word in a sentence, describing how the word and its meaning fit into that sentence.

After reading the text through once for comprehension, the teacher reads it again, but first tells the students that they should listen for the words *humorous*, *beam*, and *longingly*.

When the students hear each word, they give a thumbs-up signal. At that point the teacher stops reading and asks the students what word they heard; she then encourages them to recall the meaning of the word and how it was used in the sentence she just read. The teacher then engages the students in vocabulary activities with the word before continuing to reread the passage.

(Vocabulary words are presented in the order in which they appear in the passage; the teacher's exact words are underlined; instructions are in plain text.)

humorous	beam[ed]	longingly
Yes, *humorous* is one of our words. What does *humorous* mean? Reread the sentence with the word *humorous* in the story. If something is *humorous* what does it make you do? What are some things that you think are *humorous*?	Yes, *beamed* is one of our words. What does *beamed* mean? Reread the sentence with the word *beamed* in the story. What would make you *beam*? Why does that make you *beam*? Show me what you would look like if you were to *beam*.	Yes, *longingly* is one of our words. What does *longingly* mean? Reread the sentence with the word *longingly* in the story. When would you look at something *longingly*? How would it make you feel?
Now I will use *humorous* in a different sentence: I tried not to laugh at my friend's *humorous* faces because I didn't want to get in trouble. Now use *humorous* in your own sentence: "It was *humorous* when they _____." Guide responses as needed.	Now I will use *beamed* in a different sentence: He *beamed* as he walked up to receive his award. Now use *beamed* in your own sentence: "The girl *beamed* as she _____." Guide responses as needed.	Now I will use *longingly* in a different sentence: After playing in the hot sun all afternoon, she stared at her neighbor's glass of water *longingly*. Now use *longingly* in your own sentence: "He looked at _____ *longingly* because _____." Guide responses as needed.
Prompt students to listen for *beam[ed]* and *longingly*. Continue reading the story section.	Prompt students to listen for *longingly*. Continue reading the story section.	Continue reading to the end of the story section.

For example, on the final day of the *Chrysanthemum* (by Kevin Henkes) read-aloud, a teacher might ask students to use some of the more challenging vocabulary words they studied in an oral summary of the main points of the story. Such a summary could include responses to a series of questions designed to build oral academic language proficiency, language flexibility, and elaboration. Such questions might include the following:

- What was special about Chrysanthemum's name?
- How did she feel about her name before she went to school?
- How did her feelings about her name change after she went to school?
- What happened in the story that changed the way everyone thought about Chrysanthemum's name?
- How does Chrysanthemum feel about her name at the end of the story?
- What was your favorite part of the story? Why?

Lastly, if the book is not too long and time permits, the teacher could re-read the entire story one more time.

It is important to note that throughout the daily read-aloud lessons, and the way in which those lessons are sequenced, the main principles of vocabulary instruction for ELLs are once again reinforced. They include the following:

- Preteaching vocabulary prior to reading each day's selection, with a quick review of the previous day's words
- Active participation on the part of the student in terms of student-initiated talk, review and repetition of word meanings, and discussion about vocabulary related to the text
- Repeated read-alouds of a story, resulting in multiple exposures to targeted words

Finally, once ELLs are introduced to new vocabulary it is critical that teachers provide them with opportunities to actually use it in their everyday lives (Carlo et al., 2004; Morrow & Brittain, 2003; Vaughn-Shavuo, 1990). For example, to build proficiency in word use and contextual understanding, teachers can highlight and discuss the new vocabulary words as they are encountered again and again in other texts and in daily conversation. Beyond that, teachers can also encourage students to use these words in situations where they rely on contextualized language, such as when engaging in play, talking about life events, or expressing their desires and dislikes. For other ideas on ways teachers of primary-grade ELLs might integrate new vocabulary into everyday conversations and activities in the classroom, see Barone and Xu (2008) and Blachowicz and Fisher (2004). In this way, students gain ownership of their new vocabulary words and make them "their own," all the while building oral language proficiency (Nation, 1990) and enhancing comprehension.

Research to Practice: Reflecting on Teaching and Learning

1. With a colleague, choose two texts you would normally use for read-aloud purposes. Preview the text for Tier I, II, and III words. Make a list of words you would choose to teach to your students, depending on their levels of language proficiency and background knowledge. Create student-friendly meanings for the words. Share your choices with your colleague, justifying your selections.

2. Taking into account the important research-based elements in vocabulary instruction discussed in this chapter, consider how you might teach students a number of content-specific vocabulary such as the math terms *multiplication* and *division*.

3. Review typical sight word and high-frequency word lists, such as the Dolch Word List (Dolch, 1948) or your school district's list of grade-level vocabulary words that students are expected to know. Which words on the list do you think will be difficult to teach to ELLs? Why? Which ones will be of high interest to ELLs? How might you create meanings for those words, so that students will understand the meanings in ways presented in this chapter?

Suggestions for Further Reading

Baumann, J.F., & Kame'enui, E.J. (Eds.). (2004). *Vocabulary instruction: Research to practice.* New York: Guilford.

Beck, I.L., McKeown, M.G., & Kucan, L. (2002). *Bringing words to life: Robust vocabulary instruction.* New York: Guilford.

Calderón, M., August, D., Slavin, R., Cheung, A., Durán, D., & Madden, N. (2005). Bringing words to life in classrooms with English language learners. In A. Hiebert & M. Kamil (Eds.), *Research and development on vocabulary.* Mahwah, NJ: Erlbaum.

CHAPTER 4

Mediating Listening Comprehension

Mrs. Rodriguez:	*(first-grade dual-language general education classroom teacher) Remember, yesterday we talked about bees in our world and what we know about them. We also read the first part of our book* The Honey Makers *by Gail Gibbons and talked about what we learned. What do you remember that we learned yesterday about bees?*
Maria:	*(second-generation first-grade ELL) They are on the playground!*
Mrs. Rodriguez:	*That's right, we see them every day in our world, especially around flowers.... What is the name of their home?*
Guadalupe:	*(first-generation first-grade ELL) [Silent]*
Mrs. Rodriguez:	*Do bees live in a hive or a nest?*
Guadalupe:	*A hive!*
Mrs. Rodriguez:	*That's right, Guadalupe!*
Susana:	*(first-grade, bilingual student) They work together.*
Mrs. Rodriguez:	*Great thinking, Susana! They do work together in the hive like a giant family! Now I'm going to continue reading the next section of our book. After I'm done, I will ask each of you about what I've read. Listen carefully to the others so you can help tell what you learned.*

Mrs. Rodriguez, a teacher of ELLs who works in a suburban community just outside a larger, urban district, understands that each of her students comes to school with a unique set of experiences that informs his or her understanding of texts. Taking that into account, she uses scaffolded instruction to challenge each of them to develop greater English language proficiency.

Teachers such as Mrs. Rodriguez know that, for ELLs, comprehension of written text is inextricably linked to language proficiency (August & Shanahan, 2006). A student will have great difficulty understanding a text being read aloud if he or she is not proficient enough in the language to be able to make sense of the words or ideas being shared (Reese, Garnier, Gallimore, & Goldenberg, 2000; Royer & Carlo, 1991). Research has shown that students' level of proficiency in both their first and second languages influences the development of their English literacy skills (Reese et al., 2000). Therefore, attention to and development of students' language proficiency, through effective, integrative instruction in vocabulary and listening comprehension, is critical to advancing the literacy skills of ELLs.

The goal of this chapter is to describe ways teachers can focus students' attention on the different purposes of listening and can scaffold their instruction during strategic read-alouds in ways that target listening comprehension. Such an approach is important because it can help students build not only oral language proficiency but also important comprehension skills, such as retelling, predicting, inferring, and summarizing, that can significantly improve their academic language levels (Au, 2006; Scarcella, 2003).

Listening Comprehension Defined

Listening comprehension is the "active, conscious process in which the listener constructs meaning" from information read aloud, or from discussions taking place (O'Malley, Chamot, & Kupper, 1989, p. 434). This understanding is then applied to existing knowledge and is used either to build upon a student's schema or reconstruct faulty or incomplete understandings (O'Malley & Chamot, 1990). For ELLs, listening comprehension is a critical gateway for increasing understanding not only of the English language but also of content from text.

One of the four key areas of literacy, listening—either to gain meaning from discussion or from texts that are read aloud—is a complex skill. Students who are effective listeners engage in three active thinking processes while they are listening:

- They actively orient themselves to the task of listening and monitor their understanding of what they are hearing (Berne, 2004).
- They relate new information they hear to their prior knowledge, making "critical judgments about the value of the information" (O'Malley et al., 1989, p. 432).
- They draw inferences about "the meaning of unfamiliar words or phrases" (O'Malley et al., 1989, p. 433).

One of the important values of the read-aloud experience is that it provides multiple opportunities for teachers to help students refine these processes, in both explicit and implicit ways. One of the first and most critical ways they do that is to by orienting students to the various purposes one might have for listening to a particular passage of a text.

The Purposes of Listening to Text

The reason for students to listen to a particular text that is being read aloud depends upon the intent of the text and the meaning a teacher wants the students to gain from it. In general, there are four different types of listening comprehension: *discriminative, aesthetic, efferent,* and *critical,* each of which reflects a

Table 7. Types of Listening Comprehension

Type of listening comprehension	Purpose	Examples of use in strategic read-alouds
Discriminative	Listen to distinguish sounds	• Participate in phonemic awareness activities • Notice rhyming words in poems and songs • Recognize alliteration and onomatopoeia • Experiment with tongue twisters
Aesthetic	Listen for pleasure or enjoyment	• Listen to stories and poems read aloud • Listen for visualization
Efferent	Listen to understand a message	• Listen to gain informational from texts • Participate in instructional activities and conversations
Critical	Listen to evaluate messages	• Listen to interpret, draw inferences about, and evaluate themes and arguments

Note. From Thompkins, G. (2005). *Language arts: Patterns of practice.* Upper Saddle River, NJ: Pearson.

different reason one might listen to text (Roe & Ross, 2006; Rosenblatt, 1991; Thompkins, 2005). Table 7 lists each type, describes its purpose, and provides examples of how each is embodied in the strategic read-aloud process.

Depending on the type of text read aloud, teachers should encourage their students to focus on one or more of the different purposes for listening, such as gaining information, visualizing what the author is saying, or comparing what the author is saying with what students already know or believe to be true. At the same time, teachers need to realize that, no matter what that purpose is, students must master a similar set of comprehension skills in order to listen efficiently. Those skills include connecting new information with prior knowledge, making predictions, revising meaning and understanding while listening to a passage being read aloud, becoming familiar with different types of language, and engaging in self-monitoring (Thompkins, 2005).

The Strategic Read-Aloud as a Vehicle for Teaching Listening Comprehension

The strategic read-aloud procedure described in this book is an effective framework within which to build listening comprehension for ELLs in the primary grades (Vaughn, Cirino et al., 2006). Research has shown that read-aloud lessons not only build background knowledge and vocabulary but also contribute to the development of ELLs' listening comprehension skills and, in turn, their academic language proficiency (Anderson & Roit, 1998; Au, 1993; NICHD, 2000; Pinnell & Jaggar, 1991) by

- Providing opportunities for students to listen to texts that contain academic language
- Mediating students' listening comprehension through activities designed to explicitly draw on their background knowledge and experiences
- Explicitly reinforcing students' understanding of text structure through activities that familiarize them with concepts such as comparison and contrast, and cause and effect
- Scaffolding instruction to help students recall information from and predict events in texts they hear read aloud
- Providing opportunities for students to respond to texts they hear read aloud through related conversation and activities, thereby developing higher-level comprehension skills such as summarizing and drawing inferences

In terms of the story read-aloud instructional sequence, there are three main points at which listening comprehension can be targeted: (1) when a passage from the text is previewed and the teacher activates students' prior knowledge with respect to the content; (2) after the passage is read aloud, when teachers ask students explicit and implicit (literal and inferential) questions; and (3) following vocabulary-building activities when teachers ask open-ended questions about the story content and students respond by drawing parallels to their own lives or experiences using academic language and vocabulary from the story.

At these three points in the read-aloud, teachers focus their instruction on students' comprehension and integration of what they learn from the text, scaffolding that instruction as required. Table 8 provides an overview of how specific instructional elements are used to target listening comprehension at each of these points in the read-aloud sequence.

Prereading Activities

The importance of choosing texts purposefully, based on their cultural and experiential relevance, has already been addressed in Chapter 2; this is the first step in supporting listening comprehension. Choosing texts that align with students' experiential knowledge and schematic understanding of topics enhances listening comprehension and builds on prior knowledge. Also critical is taking

Table 8. Sequencing Read-Aloud Listening Comprehensive Activities

Before passage is read	Teachers choose a text that is aligned with a specific comprehension skill, such as comparing/contrasting or sequencing; activate students' background knowledge in relation to text content; and preview targeted vocabulary words.
After the passage is read aloud in its entirety for the first time	Teachers guide discussion of main elements of each passage for purposes of helping students comprehend text, synthesize information, make predictions, and draw inferences.
After the passage is read aloud a second time, in segments	Teachers extend comprehension through the use of instructional activities that summarize the information in the text and relate that information to students' lives.

time to introduce students to the main topic of the text and to activate their prior knowledge of that topic by previewing the targeted vocabulary words.

Activating background knowledge, also discussed in Chapter 2, is critical to developing students' understanding of textual concepts and to building schema, which in turn builds academic language proficiency. Previewing targeted vocabulary, discussed in Chapter 3, not only helps activate prior knowledge but also provides the foundation for concept and language development. Teachers using these two prereading strategies establish a strong foundation for what will come later: building on knowledge and understanding through postreading comprehension activities.

Reading Aloud

In general, there are three different approaches, or styles, to reading text aloud: (1) the co-constructed approach, involving a lot of "analytic talk during reading" (Morrow & Brittain, 2003, p. 142); (2) the didactive-interactive style, in which the teacher stops reading periodically to ask students questions; and (3) the performance-oriented approach, in which the text is read without interruption, preceded by connections to prior knowledge, and followed by questions and opportunities for students to respond (Dickinson & Smith, 1994). Research has shown that the performance-oriented approach—the model on which the strategic read-aloud procedure described in this text is based—has shown the greatest gains in listening comprehension and vocabulary acquisition (Morrow & Brittain, 2003; Vaughn, Cirino et al., 2006). Reading short passages without stopping is also the most effective strategy for building comprehension and contextual understanding of vocabulary (Morrow & Brittain, 2003).

Key to the success of the performance-oriented approach to read-alouds is the fact that both listening comprehension and vocabulary are developed in each lesson. During the first reading, the focus is on comprehension; it is during the second reading that students and teachers interact with respect to the use and meaning of new vocabulary words.

During the reading of the passage the first time, teachers can enhance the listening comprehension of ELLs by using gestures and voice intonation that emphasize especially significant words and draw attention to main ideas. Teachers can also simulate characters' voices and use props or costume items related to the passage's content as they read.

Another way for teachers to enhance listening comprehension is to emphasize what Jung (2003) refers to as discourse signaling cues, words, and phrases in the text that show relationships between ideas in a passage. As discussed in Chapter 2, these words and phrases help listeners organize the information they are hearing. According to Jung, they are used to (a) preview information (e.g., *There are four important things about whales*), (b) provide emphasis (e.g., *The most important thing about mammals is that....*), (c) summarize information learned so far (e.g., *in summary, therefore*), and (d) connect ideas (e.g., *and, but, first, second, next, however*).

Teachers can alert students to such words and phrases as they occur in the text through increased intonation or by pausing for emphasis. This strategy can be particularly effective in helping ELLs build language understanding and proficiency. Teachers might also consider targeting words serving as discourse-signaling cues as vocabulary for a given passage in the text, depending on students' language proficiency levels and the stated purpose for listening to the text.

Developing and Asking Questions

After activating background knowledge, previewing the text, and introducing three to four vocabulary words from the daily passage and their meanings, teachers set the purpose of listening with students by reminding them that a discussion of the text will follow the reading. For example, if the teacher is reading a passage from a text that lends itself to the skill of retelling, students are told that after the passage is read the first time each of them will be asked to tell what happened at the beginning, middle, and end of the passage or to restate information from the passage. That way, students are reminded of the importance of listening for the stated purpose.

Narrative works of fiction have clearly defined story sequences that are ideally suited to discussions in which students retell the story by answering the questions, Who? What? When? Where? Why? and How? But both narrative and informational texts give teachers opportunities to reinforce their students' abilities to make predictions and summarize information; if the text is culturally and experientially meaningful to the students, it also builds schema and gives students a chance to practice drawing inferences.

The role of the teacher following the initial reading of a passage is to mediate students' comprehension and oral language use by encouraging and helping them use new vocabulary and language as they respond to questions about the passage. In small groups of three to five students, each student is encouraged—and expected—to respond to such questions by contributing information that describes the overall passage or specific events in the passage. Such an approach increases individual accountability, which in turn promotes active engagement and increased opportunities to build oral language proficiency and comprehension. Teachers will want to scaffold their instruction to help ELLs with lower levels of language proficiency formulate their responses.

One way to do this would be with sentence frames that incorporate both targeted vocabulary words and story events. For example, when discussing the book *Chrysanthemum* by Kevin Henkes, the teacher might say "Chrysanthemum *beamed* when her music teacher told her that she was going to...." and then ask a student to repeat and complete the sentence with an appropriate phrase. Teachers might simply ask students with higher levels of language proficiency to respond to the question "How did Chrysanthemum feel after she met the music teacher?" in their own words. Again, regardless of a student's language proficiency level, it is critical that, as students respond to questions about the passage, teachers be prepared to scaffold their instruction as necessary to increase students' language flexibility and elaboration skills.

In larger groups, each student may not have an opportunity to participate individually. Still, all can contribute through think-pair-share strategies in which students formulate individual responses to a comprehension question, talk about their responses with a partner, and come up with one mutually-agreed-upon response. Teachers can then give students an opportunity to share their paired response with the larger group. In addition, each student is also encouraged to actively participate in the discussion by listening to their peers' responses and confirming their agreement with those responses by flashing a thumbs-up sign.

The questions teachers ask students after reading the passage should

- Align with the established purpose for listening, which is communicated prior to reading
- Reflect instruction that is scaffolded to develop each student's language proficiency level
- Reflect varied levels of questioning to help students understand the text as well as make connections to their own lives and understandings, thereby building schema

Literal and Inferential Questioning

It is at this point in the read-aloud process that listening comprehension skills are targeted for the second time. It is particularly important that teachers ask students comprehension questions that are *both* literal (the answers to which are explicit and students can find in the text) and inferential (the answers to which are implicit and which require students to make generalizations from their own experiences in order to understand the text). Such an approach helps develop a range of comprehension skills and ensures that students will make multiple connections to content.

Initially, a teacher's primary instructional goal may be for students to simply understand literal questions by being able to restate one to three main events or ideas from each text passage. This strategy is especially important for students who demonstrate lower levels of language proficiency and who may have difficulty expressing ideas in their own words or formulating responses to higher-level inferential questions. Even students with lower levels of proficiency, however, may be able—and should be encouraged—to respond to higher-level questions with brief answers.

If a story has a clear beginning, middle, and end, then a teacher might ask literal comprehension questions to elicit details about each part of the story. Alternatively, a teacher might choose to focus on story elements by asking Who? What? When? and Where? questions. Although these literal questions require students to find the answers explicitly stated in the text, they should nevertheless be structured to allow students to respond in a variety of ways and to use as much oral language flexibility as possible. In terms of inferential questions, emerging English speakers might be asked, for example, to describe, in their own words, a particular location visited by a character in the story or how a character feels based on the character's actions.

As students become more comfortable at responding to literal comprehension questions, teachers might establish a more challenging goal: helping their students answer comprehension questions that require them to draw conclusions, summarize information, and predict events. Ideally, these two types of questions—literal and inferential—should be used together, and interchangeably; in fact, once students demonstrate that they can clearly comprehend information that is stated explicitly in the text, there is no reason not to encourage them to begin drawing inferences.

What's more, as teachers pose their questions, they can capitalize on opportunities to help students develop not only their listening comprehension but also their oral language proficiency by asking them to elaborate on their initial responses or by encouraging them to answer using their "own words." In this way, particularly when working in small groups, teachers can differentiate language instruction for individual students while building comprehension and language skills for all.

For example, after reading a passage from the text, the teacher may prompt the first student with a literal question. After the student responds, the teacher might ask a second student to tell more about or add to the first student's response. Yet another student might then be asked a question that requires him to draw an inference or synthesize information that may not be included in the story but with which he or she has experience or knowledge. Clearly, this approach—asking students questions that target their individual language development needs—is a particularly effective way to scaffold—and in turn, differentiate—instruction.

Again, the type of questions asked depends to some extent on the type of text that is read aloud. For example, when the teacher is reading a work of narrative fiction, students can be asked to retell the story up to the point that the teacher stopped reading and to predict what might happen next. Questions can relate to text structure (e.g., the beginning, middle, or end of the story) or to story elements (e.g., main idea, setting, character). When the teacher is reading expository material, students can be asked to summarize information from the text or to describe the people, places, and things elaborated on in the text. Questions can relate to text structure (e.g., compare/contrast, description, cause/effect) or to the concepts introduced by the text. In both cases, vocabulary review is incorporated into questions.

Tables 9 and 10 provide examples of the kinds of listening comprehension questions that can be used to scaffold instruction for students after the first reading of a read-aloud passage. Table 9 focuses on questions based on a work of narrative fiction. Table 10 focuses on questions based on an informational, nonfiction text.

Throughout discussions about the text, the teacher's role is to extend students' thinking and oral expression by encouraging them to explain their

Table 9. Sample Listening Comprehension Questions From a Work of Narrative Fiction

- What happened first? Next? Last?
- Who was the main character?
- What do you think the word ____ means in this sentence? (Read sentence aloud to student.)
- What part of the story did you like best? Think was most interesting? Think was the funniest? Why?
- Do you sense a problem coming? Why? Why not?
- What do you think will happen next?
- Would you like to add anything to the story?
- How is this part of the story like ____?
- How is this story the same as, similar to, or different from the one we read yesterday?
- Did anything that happened with [the main character] ever happen to you? When? How was it similar?

Table 10. Sample Listening Comprehension Questions From an Informational, Nonfiction Text

- What did the author say about _____?
- Are ____ and ____ the same or different? Why?
- How are ____ and ____ the same or different? Why?
- What word did the author use to describe _____?
- If _____ is true, what do you think that would mean about _____?
- How does this information fit with what we learned about ____ yesterday?

reasoning or state concepts in different ways, using new vocabulary as appropriate. Such an approach also gives teachers valuable opportunities to informally assess students' language development.

Listening comprehension is also targeted in the second reading of the text. In reading the text for the second time, students are encouraged to extend their comprehension skills and abilities (see Tables 11, 12, and 13) by engaging in meaningful and active discussions about topics related to the text (Berne, 2004; Gersten & Baker, 2000).

In these discussions, students use academic vocabulary and language skills to discuss their own ideas about the text and connections between the text and their lives, and to elaborate on how their predictions or inferences about the text may have been confirmed or contradicted. Teachers can help facilitate such discussions by posing questions that target vocabulary words from that day's or that week's lessons; instructional scaffolding should focus on supporting students' responses and encouraging the integration of new vocabulary and elaborated responses.

Table 11. Comprehension Extension Questions for Narrative Text (English)

A Chair for My Mother (Williams, 1984)

Comprehension extension questions (Day 1, pp. 1–5)
1. What do you do after school?
2. What are some things you might want to save your money for?

Comprehension extension questions (Day 2, pp. 6–13)
1. What is the most comfortable place in your house or in your classroom, where you like to spend a lot of time?
2. How do you feel when you lose things or when things that are special to you become ruined or spoiled?

Comprehension extension questions (Day 3, pp. 13–17)
1. Have you ever had to move homes? What was it like? [or] What do you think it would be like?
2. How have you helped your neighbors or relatives? How do they help you and your family?

Comprehension extension questions (Day 4, pp. 19–end)
1. What sorts of things have you had delivered to your house or classroom?
2. Have you ever gone shopping for something big and important? What was it like? [or] What big and important thing would you like to shop for? Where would you go to find it? What would it look like, feel like, etc.?

Table 12. Comprehension Extension Questions for Informational Text (English)

Cats (Gibbons, 1996)

Comprehension extension questions (Day 1, pp. 1–7)
1. How are cats and dogs the same and different?
2. What things do mothers have to do to take care of their babies?

Comprehension extension questions (Day 2, pp. 8–12)
1. How are cats' feet the same or different from the ones people have?
2. How are cats' senses the same or different from dogs' senses?

Comprehension extension questions (Day 3, pp. 13–17)
1. How do you know when an animal is angry or happy or scared?
2. How do you know when a person is angry or happy or scared?

Comprehension extension questions (Day 4, pp. 18–23)
1. What kinds of places do you like to explore?
2. Would you rather adopt a cat or a dog? Why? If you wouldn't like to adopt a pet at all, tell why not.

Comprehension extension questions (Day 5, pp. 24–25)
1. What kind of toys might be safe for a cat?
2. What are some things that you had to learn when you were younger? What are some things you still need or want to learn?

Comprehension extension questions (Day 6, pp. 26–end)
1. What stories do you know that have cats as characters?
2. What famous cats do you know from the movies or cartoons?

Table 13. Comprehension Extension Questions for Informational Text (Spanish)

Como crecen los perritos (Selsam & Johnson, 1992)

Ampliación de comprensión (Día 1, pp. 1–11)
1. ¿Cómo son parecidos los perritos a los bebés humanos?
2. Platíqueme de un perrito que conocen.

Ampliación de comprensión (Día 2, pp. 12–29)
1. ¿Qué comen los bebés humanos?
2. ¿Son las comidas iguales o diferentes alo que comen los perritos?

Ampliación de comprensión (Día 3, pp. 29–fin)
1. ¿Conocen un perro famoso, como, de las películas? Díganme de él.
2. ¿Por qué tienen perros algunas personas? ¿Para qué sirven?

The primary instructional focus in this portion of the sequence of activities is to give students opportunities to build oral language skills; the exact nature of the skills targeted will depend upon students' language proficiency levels but generally would include language use, language flexibility, and elaboration. Thus, teachers must be careful to allow the students to do most of the talking, thereby giving them a chance to practice using language in purposeful ways.

The emphasis here is somewhat different from that of earlier activities in which students were asked to respond to literal and inferential questions posed by the teacher. Although those activities also gave students opportunities to use oral language, they focused primarily on building comprehension. Taken together, both kinds of activities combine to help increase students' content knowledge and foster academic language growth.

Balancing Content Instruction and Language Development

Effective instruction in listening comprehension for ELLs must take into account the need to balance content instruction with language development. Researchers contend that ELLs' academic literacy skills are best developed through content area instruction, an approach that builds both academic language and content knowledge (August & Hakuta, 1997; Gottlieb, 2006). It is important that when taking this approach the two goals are balanced; instruction in language development cannot be cut short to cover content, a move that could lead to lack of learning in both areas. Likewise, academic content cannot be sacrificed to build language proficiency without jeopardizing students' academic language development (Gersten & Baker, 2000).

To effectively meet both goals, careful planning must take place. Important elements of balancing the linguistic and content needs of ELLs (Gersten & Baker, 2000) include the following:

- Active student engagement in academic activities
- Frequent, daily opportunities for students to use oral language for social and academic purposes in the classroom, including "extended discourse about academic topics, and briefer responses to specific questions about content" (p. 12)
- "Building and using vocabulary as a curricular anchor" (p. 9)
- Using visual media to enhance comprehension
- Using students' native language strategically

All of these elements are part of the read-aloud procedure. For example, visuals are provided in the form of illustrations and photos from the texts being read aloud and other concrete objects teachers might use as appropriate. Students are actively engaged in comprehension and vocabulary activities following the teacher's reading of the passage. And teachers regularly provide explicit vocabulary instruction that includes the use of a student's native language, when appropriate, to increase comprehension. Students also have opportunities to use high-utility, academic vocabulary as they discuss the content of texts and make connections between that content and their own lives and experiences.

Adapting the Read-Aloud Procedure

It is important to note that the read-aloud procedure can be adapted to build a wide range of comprehension skills through the use of text structured in different ways. In fact, the National Reading Panel (NICHD, 2000) reports that students' recall of text content is increased when they are provided with explicit instruction on how to navigate a variety of text structures.

For example, through explicit instruction teachers can (a) teach students to recognize a wide range of informational text structures, such as chronological sequencing, comparison and contrast, description, and cause and effect, as well as the signal words that indicate those structures and (b) pose different types of questions suggested by each of those structures. By so doing, teachers can provide important language and content scaffolds for ELLs.

Students' understanding of text structures and comprehension of varied texts can also be strengthened through explicit instruction aimed at generalizing listening comprehension skills across content area course work (Au, 2006). In fact, teachers can use the read-aloud procedure throughout the day, selecting passages from a variety of curricular texts or trade books aligned with science, social studies, or other content areas. In this way, they can provide students with many varied opportunities to activate and reinforce their understanding of text structure and build schema while simultaneously promoting academic language development.

In conclusion, by strategically designing listening comprehension activities that relate to the stories and informational text they routinely read aloud in their classrooms, teachers can help expand both their students' conceptual knowledge and their language proficiency. In the next chapter, all of the elements and steps of the read-aloud procedure are brought together in full sample lessons that provide effective and dynamic language instruction for ELLs.

Research to Practice: Reflecting on Teaching and Learning

1. Reflect on the ways you explicitly connect language development with content knowledge development. How might you increase your attention to vocabulary and comprehension skill development during content area instruction?

2. How might you use the strategic read-aloud procedure described in this book to teach comprehension skills such as identifying the main idea or comparing and contrasting information? Which language proficiency skills outlined in your state's standards would you be simultaneously building?

3. Research has shown that providing opportunities for ELLs to work in structured peer collaboration or in structured cooperative groups can increase their language proficiency (Gersten & Baker, 2000). What are some ways this type of grouping could be used within the read-aloud procedure?

Suggested Readings for Further Study

O'Malley, J.M., & Chamot, A.U. (1990). *Learning strategies in second language acquisition.* New York: Cambridge University Press.

Thompkins, G. (2005). *Language arts: Patterns of practice* (Chapter 7: Listening to Learn). Upper Saddle River, NJ: Pearson.

Wolvin, A.D., & Coakley, C.G. (1985). *Listening* (2nd ed.). Dubuque, IA: William C. Brown.

CHAPTER 5

Putting It All Together: Sample Read-Aloud Lessons

T he previous chapters discussed important elements (grouping students, selecting texts, scaffolding language instruction in terms of tasks and materials, and developing vocabulary and comprehension) critical to the construction of the read-aloud experience for ELLs. Each was examined within the context of building schema and academic language proficiency.

The goal of this chapter is to provide sample lessons that incorporate all of these elements using equivalent texts in English and Spanish: *Julius, the Baby of the World* (Henkes, 1995) and *Julio, el rey de la casa* (Henkes & Mlawer, 1998). Equivalent texts are used to show how each lesson could progress as part of an English language arts block or in a bilingual setting in which primary reading instruction is delivered in Spanish. Teachers would use either the English or Spanish lesson depending on the language of the students' core literacy program.

Instructional Design Principles

The theoretical frameworks discussed in Chapters 1 and 2 that guided the instructional design of the strategic read-aloud procedure described in this book are summarized in Table 14. They are also reflected in the sample lessons presented in this chapter and serve as a guide to help teachers develop their own theme-based vocabulary, listening comprehension, and language-building read-aloud activities.

The sample lessons included in this chapter also reflect critical elements of effective instruction for ELLs. They include the following:

- Explicit instruction in vocabulary development, listening comprehension, and language-building skills
- Multiple exposures to explicitly targeted vocabulary words used in context to help students comprehend the themes and concepts presented in textual material

Table 14. Design Principles of the Strategic Read-Aloud Procedure

Planning considerations	Vocabulary development	Instructional scaffolding	Strategic use of language acquisition strategies
Teachers design and present read-aloud lessons that	Teachers design and present read-aloud lessons featuring activities that	Teachers design and present read-aloud lessons during which they model language and literacy skills such as	Teachers design and present read-aloud lessons that
Reflect and build upon students' level of language proficiency	Promote the development of contextual and content-specific academic and interpersonal language and vocabulary	Using flexible and elaborated language to retell a story or recall information	Integrate the use of visuals and gestures to clarify word meanings and concepts presented in the text
Address individual student learning needs			
Take place in a safe environment in which students feel comfortable taking risks in learning	Preview targeted vocabulary words	Supporting listening comprehension skills and the ability to communicate in different ways for different purposes	Provide comprehensible input to students
Take place in small groups of students, designed to promote effective language learning	Present a cumulative review of targeted vocabulary words		Incorporate the use of sentence stems and patterns to encourage student dialogue
	Provide multiple exposure to targeted vocabulary words	Using text structure to assist in text comprehension	
Are based on meaningful, interesting, and experientially relevant texts featuring comprehensible yet challenging content and appropriate levels of vocabulary, text complexity, and syntactical structures	Build contextual understanding and use of targeted vocabulary words	Making text connections across multiple readings and multiple texts	Promote active student participation in conversations about texts
		Answering literal and inferential questions	
		Summarizing the main idea	
Are thematic, linking a series of books on the same topic or augmenting a curricular unit, thereby adding depth and breadth to student knowledge and understanding		Sequencing events	
		Talking about life experiences and how they may or may not relate to text	

- Modeling of correct syntactic and semantic use of words while discussing textual content and its connection to students' life experiences
- Mediated scaffolding of instruction aligned with students' learning needs
- Language acquisition strategies that clarify concepts and promote discussions that build on and expand background knowledge and conceptual understandings

Recommended Scope and Sequence

The strategic read-aloud procedure described in this book is designed to be implemented in a five-day, recurring sequence. The suggested total time allotted for each read-aloud session is approximately 30 minutes per day and includes the following:

- Activation of prior knowledge, introduction to the text, review of previously encountered vocabulary words (if appropriate), and preteaching of new vocabulary (5–8 minutes)
- Reading aloud of one 200- to 250-word segment of the text in its entirety followed by a discussion based on literal and inferential comprehension questions (10 minutes)
- Rereading the selection a second time, stopping at each of the targeted vocabulary words and extending word knowledge and comprehension through structured, explicit activities (10 minutes)
- Summarizing the day's passage and targeted words and encouraging students to use the words in their daily experiences (1–2 minutes)

Table 15 is a week-at-a-glance chart that captures how one text, a narrative work of fiction, might be used to create five sequential strategic read-aloud lessons. Depending on the length of the text, the sequence of activities remains fairly consistent on Days 1–4, with only slight modifications needed for reviewing the text and vocabulary presented on previous days. On Day 5, or the day after the last section of the text has been read, the entire story is reread. Review again four or five of the most challenging vocabulary words from the previous four days can be reviewed once again through activities that reinforce their meanings and contextual use. Such activities might include the following:

- Using the words to create an original class story, with each student contributing a sentence that uses one of the words to the story
- Using objects to demonstrate the words

Table 15. Strategic Read-Aloud: A Week at a Glance

	Introduce story	Read passage aloud	Retell the story or summarize the text/monitoring comprehension	Reread the passage aloud in segments/focusing on vocabulary	Extend comprehension
Day 1	Solicit prior knowledge Preview Day 1 vocabulary words Establish comprehension/vocabulary goals	Use effective strategies to make content comprehensible (e.g., gestures, intonation, visuals) Emphasize target words in passage	Ask students to retell story or summarize text Ask explicit and inferential comprehension questions	Ask students to acknowledge word recognition with thumbs-up signal Review word meanings using brief activities	Extend comprehension Summarize concepts
Day 2	Review story Review targeted vocabulary words from Day 1 Preview Day 2 vocabulary words	Use effective strategies to make content comprehensible (e.g., gestures, intonation, visuals) Emphasize target words in passage	Ask students to retell story Ask explicit and inferential comprehension questions	Ask students to acknowledge word recognition with thumbs-up signal Review word meanings using brief activities	Extend comprehension Summarize concepts
Day 3	Review story Review targeted vocabulary words from Day 1 and 2 Preview Day 3 vocabulary words	Use effective strategies to make content comprehensible (e.g., gestures, intonation, visuals) Emphasize target words in passage	Ask students to retell story Ask explicit and inferential comprehension questions	Ask students to acknowledge word recognition with thumbs-up signal Review word meanings using brief activities	Extend comprehension Summarize concepts
Day 4	Review story Review targeted vocabulary words from Day 1, 2, and 3 Preview Day 4 vocabulary words	Use effective strategies to make content comprehensible (e.g., gestures, intonation, visuals) Emphasize target words in passage	Ask students to retell story Ask explicit and inferential comprehension questions	Ask students to acknowledge word recognition with thumbs-up signal Review word meanings using brief activities	Extend comprehension Summarize concepts
Day 5	Review all targeted words	Reread the entire book aloud	Ask students to retell story Ask explicit and inferential comprehension questions	Review most challenging words from the week using brief activities	Summarize concepts

- Asking students to indicate which of the targeted vocabulary words best fits in a specific sentence
- Asking students to draw a picture of one of the words to show to friends/teacher/parents
- Asking students to act out the words, perhaps by playing charades
- Asking students to orally match the words with synonyms or antonyms of the words presented by the teacher
- Making a semantic web of words that includes both the targeted word and words with similar meanings

Sample Lessons

Following are sample lessons that represent how the strategic read-aloud procedure described in this book would be used in the classroom over a four- to five-day cycle. Three sample lessons in English demonstrate how to use the read-aloud procedure on the first, second, and last day of the cycle with a narrative work of fiction, *Julius, the Baby of the World* by Kevin Henkes (1995). An additional sample lesson for Day 1 is presented in Spanish using *Julio, el rey de la casa* (Henkes & Mlawer, 1998), the Spanish version of the same book.

It is important to note that these two texts would not be read simultaneously with the same group of students; that is, the English text would be read when students receive their core literacy instruction in English (i.e., in ESL or resource classrooms or in classrooms in which students were learning literacy in English). The Spanish text would be read when students receive their core literacy instruction in Spanish (i.e., in their bilingual general education classroom or bilingual literacy resource classroom).

Note, too, that the vocabulary words that are targeted for explicit instruction from the English version of the text differ significantly from those chosen from the Spanish version. That's because teachers would generally choose more advanced, higher-level vocabulary words to extend students' native language than they would choose to extend their second language.

Finally, in the sample lessons presented, the teacher's words are printed in italics. Directions for the teacher are in normal font. Suggestions for scaffolding instruction are in boldface font.

FAMILIES—DAY 1 (ENGLISH)

Materials
- *Julius, the Baby of the World* (pages 1–5) by Kevin Henkes (1995)

- Stopwatch or simple timer (for monitoring pace)
- Vocabulary word cards: Three 4" x 6" index cards with one of the following targeted vocabulary words and its corresponding meaning written on opposite sides of each card:

> **insulting** (*adj*), mean or rude
>
> **admire** (*v*), to think something is special, good or beautiful
>
> **disgusting** (*adj*), awful, horrible

Introduce the story and three to four Tier II vocabulary words (3 minutes)

1. Introduce the theme of the book to the students. Remind the students of other times they have encountered the same theme. Show the cover of the book and first page of the story to students. Read the title and present the main elements of the story.

   Today we are going to read the first of three stories that are about families. The title of today's story is Julius, the Baby of the World. *It was written by a man named Kevin Henkes. He is the author. This story is about a little girl named Lilly and her new baby brother.*

2. Access prior knowledge and build background experiences.

   Do any of you have younger brothers, sisters, cousins, or friends? What is it like having a younger brother, sister, cousin, or friend? If you don't have younger brothers or sisters, what do you think it would be like to live with a baby in the house?

   Scaffold instruction to encourage students' dialogue or language use by

   • Providing an example from your [teacher's] life experience.

   • Providing an oral language stem: *My brother is very _____.*

   When I had a baby sister, the house was always noisy because she cried a lot. What are some things that babies do?

3. Introduce new vocabulary.

   Today, you will listen for three new words in the story.

   - Show the word card. *The first word is* insulting. *What is the word?* [Students should repeat the word after the teacher.]

   - Read the definition. *The word* insulting *means mean or rude.*

   - Repeat these steps for the words *admired* and *disgusting.*

Read aloud for comprehension (8 minutes)

1. Direct students to listen to the story as it is read aloud, establish the purpose for listening.

   Now I will read Julius, the Baby of the World. *Then I will ask you questions about what I've read. Listen carefully for the words* insulting, admired, *and* disgusting *as I read.*

2. Read the entire section without stopping (pp. 1–5). Read with appropriate pacing, enunciation, intonation, gestures, and mime if appropriate.

3. Ask students to retell the story using vocabulary words.

   I will ask one student at a time about what I've read. Listen carefully to the others so you can help retell the story. Try to use our new words when you can.

4. Select an individual student to retell what happened in the story.

   In your own words, tell me what happened in this part of the story.

   Scaffold instruction by
   - **Showing pictures from the book to help students recall information**
   - **Using question words such as *who, what, when, where,* and *why* to elicit information**
   - **Using words that suggest sequential order, such as *first, next,* and *last***

5. Ask a different student to build upon the first student's response.

   Scaffold instruction by using open-ended questions, probing for additional information.
   - *How did Lilly treat Julius after he was born?*
   - *How did her parents treat him?*

6. Ask another student an inferential question, probing for more implicit information.

   Scaffold instruction by using open-ended questions, probing for additional information:
   - *Why do you think Lilly's feelings about Julius changed after he was born?*
   - *What do you think might happen next?*
   - *How do you think Lilly felt about having a baby brother before Julius was born?*
   - *How does she feel once baby Julius is living at home?*

Reread the story (5 minutes)

1. Display the three new vocabulary words.

   Let's review our new words. Say the word after me and tell us what the word means. The first word was _____. Say it. What does _____ mean?

   [Students repeat and define each of the three words.]

   I will read the story again. This time listen for the three words. When you hear one, show me the thumbs-up sign like this.

   [Teacher models the sign.]

2. Begin reading the story a second time. As you read the first vocabulary word, look to see if students have their thumbs up. If not, stop reading and tell the students that one of the vocabulary words was in the previous sentence. Tell them you will read the sentence again and ask them to put their thumbs up when they hear the word. If they do not identify the word the second time you read the sentence, tell them the word and read it in the sentence a third time, modeling the thumbs-up sign and asking them to show you their sign.

3. When students give the signal, stop reading.

   I see you have your thumbs up. Which of the new words did you hear?

   [Students say word.]

   Point to the word and remove the card. Continue with the dialogue provided in Table 16.

Extend comprehension (5 minutes)

The goal of this part of the lesson is to engage the students in a discussion during which they use the targeted vocabulary words. The teacher's role is to begin the discussion with conversation starters and to prompt students, as necessary, to ask one another questions. However, students should do the majority of the talking. Such a discussion could focus on the students' thoughts and opinions about what it's like to have a brother or sister.

1. *Tell me about your brother or sister.* (Or, for children who do not have a brother or sister, *Do you have a cousin or neighbor you play with? How do you play together?*)

2. *Are there any new babies in your family or in your house? Tell us what it is like to be around a new baby.*

Summarize concepts (1 minute)

Today we began reading Julius, the Baby of the World. *You did a great job listening to the story and remembering the words* insulting, admired, *and* disgusting.

Table 16. Sample Dialogue for New Vocabulary (English)

insulting	admired	disgusting
A. *Yes,* insulting *is one of our words. What does* insulting *mean?* Reread the sentence from the story that includes the word *insulting.* *How does it feel when someone says something that is* insulting? *Would you want someone to say something* insulting *to you?* B. *Now I will use* insulting *in a different sentence:* *My mother says we may not say* insulting *things to each other on the playground.* *Now use* insulting *in your own sentence.* Guide responses as needed. **To scaffold instruction:** ***Now complete this sentence:*** ***I feel _____ when someone does something that is insulting.*** Prompt students to listen for *admired* and *disgusting.* Continue reading the story section.	A. *Yes,* admired *is one of our words. What does* admired *mean?* Reread the sentence from the story that includes the word *admired.* *Who is someone you* admire? *What do you* admire *about them?* B. *Now I will use* admired *in a different sentence:* *I* admired *the way my friend could do tricks on his skateboard.* *Now use* admired *in your own sentence.* Guide responses as needed. **To scaffold instruction:** ***Now complete this sentence:*** ***I admired _____ because he/she can _____.*** Prompt students to listen for *disgusting.* Continue reading the story section.	A. *Yes,* disgusting *is one of our words. What does* disgusting *mean?* Reread the sentence from the story that includes the word *disgusting.* *What are some things that you think would be/are* disgusting? B. *Now I will use* disgusting *in a different sentence:* *The cold soup we had for lunch had a* disgusting *taste.* *Now use* disgusting *in your own sentence.* Guide responses as needed. **To scaffold instruction:** ***Now complete this sentence:*** ***Food that is covered with _____ is disgusting.*** Continue reading to the end of the story section.

Listen for these words when you hear stories or when adults are talking. Try to use these words when you talk to other people.

Instruction on Days 2, 3, and 4 of the lesson follow much the same sequence as that of Day 1, with additional vocabulary words each day and a quick review of the previous day's vocabulary. Again, Table 15 (on page 74) summarizes the format the lessons take on each of those days.

FAMILIAS—DÍA 1 (SPANISH)

Materiales

• *Julius, el rey de la casa* (páginas 1–8) por Henkes & Mlawer (1998)
• Un cronómetro (para marcar la pauta de la lección)

- Las palabras de vocabulario: Tres tarjetas índice con una de las palabras de vocabulario de esta lección, y su significado escrito en el lado opuesto de cada targeta

> **pellizcaba** *(v)*, apretar la piel con el dedo pulgar y otro dedo
>
> **adorable** *(adj)*, chulo, precioso
>
> **asqueroso** *(adj)*, horrible

Introduzca el cuento y las tres palabras académicas de vocabulario (3 minutos)

1. Les introduzca el tema del libro, si es nuevo, a los estudiantes. Si no es nuevo, repase con ellos otras veces en las que encontraron el mismo tema. Les enseñe el cubierto del libro y la primera página del cuento a ellos. Lea el título y describa las ideas principales del cuento.

   Hoy leemos el primer libro de nuestro tema de familias. Hay tres libros en este tema. El título del cuento de hoy es "Julius el rey de la casa." Fue escrito por el autor Kevin Henkes y Teresa Mlawer. El cuento se trata de una niña llamada Lilly y sus experiencias con su hermano nuevo, Julius.

2. Pregunte sobre conocimientos y experiencias anteriores.

   ¿Tienes un/a hermano/a menor? O si no, ¿Tienes un primo o amigo menor? ¿Cómo es?

   Se les apoye su aprendizaje del diálogo o uso del lenguaje de los estudiantes por

   • Darles un ejemplo de sus experiencias sobre este tema.

   • Darles una frase corto para completar a su nivel del lenguaje: Mi hermano es muy _____.

   Cuando era chiquita mi hermanita, siempre había mucho ruido porque lloraba mucho. ¿Qué son las cosas que hacen los bebés?

3. Les introduzca a las palabras nuevas de vocabulario.

   Hoy escuchen atentamente durante el cuento para que puedan identificar las tres palabras de vocabulario.

   • Enséñeles la primera tarjeta de vocabulario. *La primera palabra es* pellizcaba. *¿Qué es?* [Se les apoye a los estudiantes repetir la palabra.]

   • Lea el significado de la palabra. Pellizcaba *significa apretar la piel con el dedo pulgar y otro dedo.*

   • Repita estos pasos incorporando las palabras *adorable* y *asqueroso.*

Lea y comprenda (8 minutos)

1. Les dirija a los estudiantes escuchar a Ud. mientras lea el cuento. Dígales de la intención de escuchar.

   Ahora leeré Julius, el rey de la casa. *Después, les haré unas preguntas sobre el cuento. Escuchen atentamente para poder identificar las palabras* pellizcaba, adorable, *y* asqueroso, *mientras que yo lea.*

2. Lea la primera parte del cuento sin parar (pp. 1–8). Lea con ritmo, enunciación, y entonación.

3. Anime a los estudiantes a que usen palabras de vocabulario al recontar el cuento.

   Le preguntaré a cada uno (uno a la vez) cosas sobre el cuento. Escuchen atentamente para que puedan ayudar a recontar el cuento. Por favor, se trate de usar las palabras nuevas cuando pueda.

4. Seleccione a un alumno a usar una descripción explícita para recontar lo que pasó en esta parte del cuento.

   En tus propias palabras, resume lo que sucedió en esta parte del cuento.

   Si es necesario, se les apoye a su comprensión por

   - **Enseñarles las ilustraciones del cuento para ayudarles recontar la información**
   - **Pregúntele sobre las características del cuento:** *quién, qué, dónde,* **y** *cuándo* **para solicitar más información.**
   - **Use palabras para señalar la secuencia del cuento, como** *primero, el próximo,* **y** *al fin.*

5. Pida a un alumno distinto que use la respuesta de su compañero de clase para reforzar su propia respuesta.

   Si es necesario, se les apoye a su comprensión por preguntarles como las siguientes:

   - **¿Después de su nacimiento, cómo les trababa Lilly a Julius?**
   - **¿Cómo lo trataban sus padres?**

6. Pregúntele a otro estudiante una pregunta deductiva para obtener más información.

   Si es necesario, se les apoye a su comprensión por

- *¿Por qué cambiaron los sentimientos de Lilly acerca de su hermano después de su nacimiento?*
- *¿Qué piensas que ocurrirá?*
- *¿Cómo se siente Lilly tener un hermano menor, antes de que nació él?*

Lea el cuento de nuevo (5 minutos)

1. Enseñe las tres palabras de vocabulario.

    Repitan las palabras de vocabulario y den la definición de cada palabra: pellizcaba, adorable, y asqueroso. La primera palabra es _____. ¿Qué significa?

    [Los estudiantes repiten y dan la definición de las palabras de vocabulario.]

    Leeré el cuento de nuevo. Esta vez quiero que pongan atención a las palabras de vocabulario. Cuando ustedes oigan una de las palabras, apunten el dedo pulgar hacia arriba.

    [Demuestre la señal.]

2. Inicie a leer el cuento por la segunda vez. Cuando encuentre la primera palabra de vocabulario, vea hacia los alumnos para estar seguro a que tienen el dedo pulgar hacia arriba. Si no, pare y dígales a los alumnos que se encuentra una de las palabras nuevas de vocabulario en la frase anterior. Dígales que leerá la frase de nuevo, y pídales que usen el modelo del dedo pulgar hacia arriba cuando oigan la palabra. Si todavía no identifican la palabra, diga la palabra y lea la frase de nuevo, enseñándoles la señal y pidiéndoles que le copien a Ud.

3. Cuando los estudiantes hagan la señal, pare y diga:

    Veo que tienen el dedo pulgar hacia arriba. [Escoja un estudiante.] *¿Cuál de las palabras nuevas oíste?*

    [El estudiante dice la palabra.]

    Señale con el dedo pulgar y quite la tarjeta. Siga con el diálogo y las actividades de vocabulario en Table 17.

Ampliación de comprensión (5 minutes)

La meta de esta parte de la lección es tener una discusión con los estudiantes en la cual usen las palabras de vocabulario nuevo de la lección. El papel del maestro/a es empezar la discusión con preguntas y apoyarles discutir y preguntar sobre sus pensamientos y opiniones sobre las temas en esta parte del cuento, entre sí. Pregúnteles las siguientes preguntas y deje suficiente tiempo para que cada estudiante responda. Ayúdeles cuando es necesario, pidiendo

Table 17. Sample Dialogue for New Vocabulary (Spanish)

pellizcaba	adorable	asqueroso
A. *Sí, pellizcaba es una de nuestras palabras. ¿Qué quiere decir pellizcaba?* Lea de nuevo la oración en cual la palabra *pellizcaba* se encuentra. *¿Te gusta que alguien te pellizque? ¿Qué otros usos tiene la acción de pellizcar en vez de hacer daño?* B. *Ahora uso pellizcaba en otra oración: Para poner el hilo en la aguja, pellizcaba el hilo con fuerza. Ahora formen sus propias oraciones usando pellizcaba.* **Les apoye si es necesario: Completa la siguiente frase: Para _____, pellizcaba al/ a la _____.** Anime a los estudiantes que pongan atención a las palabras *adorable* y *asqueroso*. Siga leyendo el cuento. Repita pasos 2 y 3 con las otras dos palabras. Escoja a un estudiante distinto cada vez.	A. *Sí, adorable es una de nuestras palabras. ¿Qué quiere decir* adorable? Lea de nuevo la oración que tiene la palabra *adorable* en el cuento. B. *Ahora uso adorable en una oración distinta: Mi perrito Mac es adorable. Ahora formen su propia oración con la palabra adorable.* **Les apoye si es necesario. Completa la siguiente frase: Pienso que ____ es una cosa adorable.** Anime a los estudiantes que pongan atención a la palabra *asqueroso*. Siga leyendo el cuento.	A. *Sí, asqueroso es una de nuestras palabras. ¿Qué quiere decir* asqueroso? Lea de nuevo la oración que tiene la palabra *asqueroso* en el cuento. B. *Ahora uso asqueroso en una oración distinta: El bote de basura está asqueroso. Ahora formen su propia oración con la palabra asqueroso.* **Les apoye si es necesario. Completa la siguiente frase: El ____ está asqueroso (porque _____).** Siga leyendo el cuento hasta p. 8.

más información. Los estudiantes deben ser los que están hablando, no la maestra, para la mayoría del tiempo sobre el tema de tener un hermanito nuevo:

1. *Díganme de unos de sus hermanos, primos, o amigos y como juegan entre sí.*

2. *¿Cómo se tratan a los bebés?*

Repaso del cuento y palabras (1 minuto)

Hoy leímos Julius el rey de la casa. *Su empeño en escuchar y recordar las palabras pellizcaba, asqueroso y adorable fue excelente. Recuerden estas palabras cuando lean un cuento o cuando escuchen a los adultos conversar.*

Conclusion

According to Neuman (2006), "For early education to work toward helping children to attain social and economic equality, we must develop pedagogy that is both sensitive to children's development and representative of conceptual knowledge" (p. 38). Researchers also contend that children who are raised in homes where the primary language is not English have "language and literacy experiences that are very different from those of their...peers" (Wasik, Bond, & Hindman, 2005, p. 91).

This chapter provides an overview and template teachers can use to design their daily read-aloud sessions in ways that speak to both those issues. The goal is to enhance the oral language development—and, specifically, comprehension and academic vocabulary development—of ELLs. Structuring read-aloud lessons to include the elements addressed in these chapters can contribute to language and literacy development by transporting children to new places of knowledge and language experience. When teachers engage their students in listening to narrative texts that relate to and expand upon their experiences, or informational texts that build knowledge of material of interest to them, they are taking important steps to increase their students' literacy skills. Additionally, for some students the experience also will lead to a lifelong love of books and reading.

Without such interactions with texts and language, ELLs will be forever and significantly limited in their ability to access critical information and knowledge and less likely to develop the positive dispositions toward texts and reading that are necessary for academic success. Only by providing dynamic, rich, scaffolded opportunities to interact with books can we hope to narrow the persistent and limiting achievement disparities for ELLs.

Research to Practice: Reflecting on Teaching and Learning

1. Did you plan lessons that built on students' prior knowledge and experiences and provided mediated scaffolds for students' varying levels of oral language proficiency?

2. Did you teach new target words prior to reading the story?

3. Did you scaffold instruction with gestures, visuals from the text, and other language learning strategies to assist students who were not orally proficient?

4. Did you allow students to retell the story or summarize the text and encourage other students to expand upon their responses?

5. Did you encourage students to use target words in retelling the story or when talking about books?

6. Did you create opportunities for all students to contribute to the retelling of the story or summarizing of the text?

7. Did you allow time for cumulative review of newly taught words and concepts?

8. Did you encourage students to use new words from the text to describe their own life experiences?

Suggested Readings for Further Study

Neuman, S.B. (2006). The knowledge gap: Implications for early education. In S.B. Neuman & D.K. Dickinson (Eds.), *Handbook of early literacy research* (pp. 29–40). New York: Guilford.

Lubeck, S. (1996). Deconstructing "child development knowledge" and "teacher preparation." *Early Childhood Research Quarterly, 11*(2), 147–167.

Wasik, B.A., Bond, M.A., & Hindman, A. (2005). Educating at-risk students from preschool through high school. *Yearbook of the National Society for the Study of Education, 101*(2), 89–110.

Research Basis for the Strategic Read-Aloud Procedure

As practicing teachers, we live in an educational climate in which we are urged to make decisions about the instructional practices we use based on the extent to which they are supported by empirical evidence. Thus, it would be wise to ask, "What research basis is there for the strategic read-aloud procedure described in this book?"

The procedure is based on the results of four separate intervention studies—two in English and two in Spanish—we conducted with ELLs. The results of all four studies (Vaughn, Linan-Thompson et al., 2006; Vaughn, Mathes et al., 2006; Vaughn, Mathes, Linan-Thompson, & Francis, 2005; Vaughn, Cirino et al., 2006) have been published.

The studies were conducted as part of a broader, longitudinal study of 1,400 Spanish-speaking students in Texas and California during the 2002–2003 academic year (Vaughn, Cirino et al., 2006; for more information see the Development of English Literacy with Spanish Speakers—DELSS website www.cal.org/delss/#GRANTS).

In each study, the strategic read-aloud procedure we describe in this book was used to maximize comprehension and oral vocabulary development in first-grade students learning to read in either Spanish or English who were at risk of developing reading problems. By matching the language of the intervention with the language of the students' core reading instruction, students received 50 minutes of daily reading instruction from a trained bilingual teacher in English or Spanish. It was within the context of designing these studies that the strategic read-aloud procedure we describe in this book was developed.

Overview of Intervention Studies: English and Spanish

The students who participated in the interventions were from elementary schools located in geographical locations with a high density of ELLs: two urban school districts in Texas and one district located along the Texas–Mexico border. In general, these schools were selected based on specific criteria, including (a) average or above-average third-grade state accountability data, (b) free- or reduced-lunch eligibility of 60% or more of total enrollment, and (c) Latino enrollment of 60% or more. Four of the schools in the study were rated as exemplary and three as recognized based on student performance on state accountability measures. As a result, we concluded that the schools were successful in providing literacy instruction to most students on campus and were teaching students to read in environments conducive to learning (Vaughn et al., 2003).

Two waves of first-grade students participated in the intervention studies. During each data wave, students were provided English or Spanish interventions based on the language in which they received their core reading instruction. Students participated in either the first (Cohort 1 Spanish and Cohort 1 English) or second (Cohort 2 Spanish and Cohort 2 English) wave of intervention studies; they were recruited from the same schools in the same cities and met the same screening criteria. The first set of intervention studies took place during the 2002–2003 school year; the second set of studies took place during the following school year with a new wave of first graders to further validate the findings.

Students were eligible to participate in the interventions based on their ability to identify letters and read words in Spanish and English as measured by the Letter/Word Identification subtest from the Woodcock Language Proficiency Battery-Revised (WLPB-R; Woodcock, 1991) at the beginning of the school year. In general, eligible students shared several characteristics: they (a) were unable to read more than one word on a word-reading screening measure, (b) scored below the 25th percentile on the Letter/Word Identification first-grade subtest of the WLPB, and (c) demonstrated low oral language proficiency in Spanish and English.

Students were assigned randomly, by language of core reading instruction, to either a Spanish intervention group or a contrast group that received no intervention ($N = 65$ for Year 01; $N = 94$ for Year 02), or to an English intervention group or a contrast group that received no intervention ($N = 41$ for Year 01; $N = 91$ for Year 02). All students continued to receive their core reading instruction from their reading teacher. It is important to note, however, that instruction delivered through the intervention did not supplant or interfere with the typical reading instruction provided to these students from their core reading teacher.

The participants and findings for each cohort have been described in published research studies; only an overview of findings is presented here (Vaughn, Linan-Thompson et al., 2006; Vaughn, Mathes et al., 2006).

The Teachers and Curriculum

Teachers of both the Spanish and English interventions were bilingual (Spanish/English) and received professional development in the intervention at the beginning of the year; they also received ongoing training, coaching, and videotaping with feedback throughout the year from study researchers. Teachers provided daily, intensive, systematic instruction to small groups of three to five students for 50 minutes a day over a period of seven months.

The instruction followed specially designed curricula written in English (Mathes, Torgesen, Wahl, Menchetti, & Grek, 1999) and in Spanish (Mathes, Linan-Thompson, Pollard-Durodola, Hagan, & Vaughn, 2003). The curricula incorporated research-based components reflecting current theories on how students learn to read in a transparent alphabetic language such as Spanish (e.g., a language that features consistent letter–sound mappings) or in an opaque orthography language such as English (e.g., a language that features inconsistent letter–sound correspondence). Although both curricula used the same design principles of explicit instruction (e.g., teacher modeling, guided group practice, and individual practice/mastery of concepts; Carnine, Silbert, & Kame'enui, 1997), they were not translations of each other and were tailored to meet the needs of students learning to read in two different languages.

The first 40 minutes of the 50 minutes of daily instruction included 6–10 short activities, integrating simple to complex skills across several instructional strands: phonemic awareness, letter knowledge, word study (decoding and encoding), reading connected text, reading comprehension, and fluency-building (Vaughn et al., 2005; Vaughn, Cirino et al., 2006; Vaughn, Mathes et al., 2006). The strategic read-aloud procedure on which this text is based was taught in Spanish or English for the last 10 minutes.

The Strategic Read-Aloud Component of the Intervention Studies

Because students eligible for the supplemental interventions were not proficient in either Spanish or English as indicated by low language proficiency scores in both languages, we developed a systematic instructional approach to supporting their oral language development through a framework that included (a) engaging students in oral language development activities, (b) selecting vocabulary words for instruction at students' level of proficiency, (c) teaching new words within the context of familiar concepts embedded within highly appealing text, and (d) improving listening comprehension skills.

The Study Findings

After seven months of daily intensive reading instruction in English, students in the English intervention cohort outperformed students in the contrast group in the area of phonological awareness, letter and sound knowledge, word attack, spelling dictation, and passage comprehension (Vaughn, Mathes et al., 2006). Effect sizes in favor of the students in the English intervention cohort over students in the contrast group included d = 1.24 for phonological awareness composite score, 1.09 for word attack, and 1.08 for passage comprehension. For a discussion of effect sizes and their definitions, see Cohen (1988). In general, effect sizes of 0.2 are considered small; 0.5, moderate; 0.8 or above, large.

The most significant finding was that students in the English intervention cohort made greater gains in the area of reading comprehension than monolingual English-speaking students who received instruction using the same English curriculum in an intervention study conducted by Mathes et al. (2003). The difference between the two literacy interventions that were delivered in English (the one on which this book is based, conducted with ELLs, and the one studied by Mathes et al., conducted with monolingual, English-speaking students) was the addition of the strategic read-aloud component with the ELLs.

Furthermore, ELLs randomly placed in the contrast group who did not receive the intervention demonstrated very little gain in reading comprehension; they achieved an average pretest standard score of 82 and posttest mean standard score of 84 (Vaughn, Mathes et al., 2006).

Literacy gains were also impressive among members of the Spanish intervention cohort, who outperformed students in the contrast group in the area of phonemic awareness, word attack, word reading, reading comprehension, fluency, and language development in Spanish (Vaughn, Linan-Thompson et al., 2005). Effect sizes in favor of the treatment students over comparison students in Spanish ranged from d = 0.35 for oral language composite in Spanish to 0.85 for word attack.

In an attempt to explain between-group differences in favor of student in the intervention cohorts, researchers suggested that due to the orthographic transparency of the Spanish language, students were able to use consistent letter–sound mappings to read more complex word and text structures earlier, allowing students to focus progressively on more difficult comprehension strategies (Vaughn, Linan-Thompson et al., 2006). In support of this explanation, Mathes et al. (2003) emphasize that the at-risk students in the Spanish intervention cohort were able to read more complex text structures earlier than monolingual English-speaking students who were also at risk for reading failure.

Findings from the Spanish intervention study also suggest that the addition of the strategic read-aloud element that focused on developing vocabulary, listening comprehension, and general oral language skills may have accounted for the dramatic increase in text comprehension seen in students by the end of the year (Vaughn, Linan-Thompson, Mathes et al., 2006).

Both sets of intervention studies support findings by previous researchers that relate students' vocabulary knowledge to reading ability and comprehension (Biemiller, 2003; Carlo et al., 2004; Hickman, Pollard-Durodola, & Vaughn, 2004; McLaughlin, 1987; NICHD, 2000; Snow, Burns, & Griffin, 1998).

REFERENCES

Anderson, V., & Roit, M. (1996). Linking reading comprehension instruction to language development for language-minority students. *The Elementary School Journal, 96*(3), 295–309. doi:10.1086/461829

Anderson, V., & Roit, M. (1998). Reading as a gateway to language proficiency for language-minority students in the elementary grades. In R.M. Gersten & R.T. Jiménez (Eds.), *Promoting learning for culturally and linguistically diverse students: Classroom applications from contemporary research* (pp. 42–54). Belmont, CA: Wadsworth.

Au, K.H. (1993). *Literacy instruction in multicultural settings.* New York: Harcourt.

Au, K.H. (2006). *Multicultural issues and literacy achievement.* Mahwah, NJ: Erlbaum.

August, D. (2002). *Transitional programs for English language learners: Contextual factors and effective programming.* Baltimore: Center for Research on the Education of Students Placed at Risk.

August, D. (2003). *Supporting the development of English literacy in English language learners: Key issues and promising practices.* Baltimore: Center for Research on the Education of Students Placed at Risk.

August, D., Beck, I.L., Calderón, M., Francis, D.J., Lesaux, N.K., Shanahan, T. (with Erickson, F., & Siegel, L.S.). (2008). Instruction and professional development. In D. August & T. Shanahan (Eds.), *Developing reading and writing in second-language learners* (pp. 131–250). New York: Routledge.

August, D., Calderón, M., & Carlo, M. (2002). *Transfer of skills from Spanish to English: A study of young learners.* Washington, DC: Center for Applied Linguistics.

August, D., Carlo, M., Dressler, C., & Snow, C. (2005). The critical role of vocabulary development for English language learners. *Learning Disabilities Research & Practice, 20*(1), 50–57. doi:10.1111/j.1540-5826.2005.00120.x

August, D., & Hakuta, K. (Eds.). (1997). *Improving schooling for language-minority children: A research agenda.* Washington, DC: National Academy Press.

August, D., & Shanahan, T. (2006). *Developing literacy in second-language learners: Report of the National Literacy Panel on Language Minority Children and Youth.* Mahwah, NJ: Erlbaum.

August, D., & Shanahan, T. (2008). Introduction and methodology. In D. August & T. Shanahan (Eds.), *Developing reading and writing in second-language learners* (pp. 1–18). New York: Routledge.

Barone, D.M., & Xu, S.H. (2008). *Literacy instruction for English language learners, pre-K–2.* New York: Guilford.

Barrera, R.B. (1992). The cultural gap in literature-based literacy instruction. *Education and Urban Society, 24*(2), 227–243. doi:10.1177/0013124592024002005

Beck, I.L., McKeown, M.G., & Kucan, L. (2002). *Bringing words to life: Robust vocabulary instruction.* New York: Guilford.

Berne, J.E. (2004). Listening comprehension strategies: A review of the literature. *Foreign Language Annals, 37*(4), 521–533.

Biemiller, A. (2003). Teaching vocabulary in the primary grades: Vocabulary instruction needed. In J.F. Baumann and E.J. Kame'enui (Eds.), *Reading vocabulary: Research to practice* (pp. 28–40). New York: Guilford

Blachowicz, C.L.Z., & Fisher, P. (2004). Keep the "fun" in fundamental: Encouraging word awareness and incidental word learning in the classroom through word play. In J.F. Baumann & E.J. Kame'enui (Eds.), *Vocabulary instruction: Research to practice* (pp. 218–238). New York: Guilford.

Blok, H. (1999). Reading to young children in educational settings: A meta-analysis of recent research. *Language Learning, 49*(2), 343–371.

Brinton, D.M., Snow, M.A., & Wesche, M.B. (1993). Content-based second language instruction. In J.W. Oller Jr. (Ed.), *Methods that work: Ideas for literacy and language teachers* (2nd ed., pp. 136–142). Boston: Heinle & Heinle.

Calderón, M., August, D., Slavin, R., Duran, D., Madden, N., & Cheung, A. (2005). Bringing words to life in classrooms with English-language learners. In E.H. Hiebert & M.L. Kamil (Eds.), *Teaching and learning vocabulary: Bringing research to practice* (pp. 115–136). Mahwah, NJ: Erlbaum.

Carlo, M.S., August, D., McLaughlin, B., Snow, C.E., Dressler, C., Lippman, D., et al. (2004). Closing the gap: Addressing the vocabulary needs of English-language learners in bilingual and mainstream classrooms. *Reading Research Quarterly, 39*(2), 188–215. doi:10.1598/RRQ.39.2.3

Carnine, D.W., Silbert, J., & Kame'enui, E.J. (1997). *Direct instruction reading* (3rd ed.). Upper Saddle River, NJ: Prentice-Hall.

Chamot, A.U., & O'Malley, J.M. (1994). Instructional approaches and teaching procedures. In K. Spangenberg-Urbschat & R. Pritchard (Eds.), *Kids come in all languages: Reading instruction for ESL students* (pp. 82–107). Newark, DE: International Reading Association.

Cohen, J. (1988). *Statistical power analysis for the behavioral sciences* (2nd ed.). Hillsdale, NJ: Erlbaum.

Collier, V.P. (1987). Age and rate of acquisition of second language for academic purposes. *TESOL Quarterly, 21*(4), 617–641. doi:10.2307/3586986

Collier, V.P. (1989). How long? A synthesis on research on academic achievement in a second language. *TESOL Quarterly, 23*(3), 509–531. doi:10.2307/3586923

Collier, V.P. (1995). *Promoting academic success for all ESL students: Understanding second language acquisition for school.* Jersey City, NJ: New Jersey Teachers of English to Speakers of Other Languages-Bilingual Educators.

Cummins, J. (1984). *Bilingualism and special education: Issues in assessment and pedagogy.* Clevedon, UK: Multilingual Matters.

Cummins, J. (1994). The acquisition of English as a second language. In K. Spangenberg-Urbschat & R. Pritchard (Eds.), *Kids come in all languages: Reading instruction for ESL students* (pp. 36–62). Newark, DE: International Reading Association.

Dickinson, D.K., & Smith, M.W. (1994). Long-term effects of preschool teachers' book readings on low-income children's vocabulary and story comprehension. *Reading Research Quarterly, 29*(2), 104–122. doi:10.2307/747807

Dolch, E.W. (1948). *Problems in reading.* Campaign, IL: Garrard Press.

Duke, N.K. (1999). *Using nonfiction to increase reading achievement and word knowledge.* Occasional paper of the Scholastic Center for Literacy and Learning, New York.

Duke, N.K. (2000). 3.6 minutes per day: The scarcity of informational texts in first grade. *Reading Research Quarterly, 35*(2), 202–224. doi:10.1598/RRQ.35.2.1

Duke, N.K., Bennett-Armistead, V.S., & Roberts, E.M. (2003). Filling the nonfiction void: Why we should bring nonfiction into the early-grade classroom. *American Educator, 27*(1), 30–34.

Edelsky, C. (1990). *With literacy and justice for all: Rethinking the social in language and education.* London: Falmer.

Ellis, R. (1990). *Instructed second language acquisition: Learning in the classroom.* Oxford: Blackwell.

Federal Interagency Forum on Child and Family Statistics. (2002). *America's children: Key national indicators of well-being.* Federal Interagency Forum on Child and Family Statistics. Washington, DC: U.S. Government Printing Office.

Fitzgerald, J. (1995). English as a second language reading instruction in the United States: A research review. *Journal of Reading Behavior, 27*(2), 115–152.

García, G.E., Montes, J.A., Janisch, C., Bouchereau, E., & Consalvi, J. (1993). Literacy needs of limited-English proficient students: What information is available to mainstream teachers? In D.J. Leu & C.K. Kinzer (Eds.), *Examining central issues in literacy research, theory, and practice* (42nd yearbook of the National Reading Conference, pp. 171–178). Chicago: National Reading Conference.

Gersten, R., & Baker, S. (2000). What we know about effective instructional practices of English-language learners. *Exceptional Children, 66*(4), 454–470.

Gersten, R., Baker, S.K., & Marks, S.U. (1999). *Teaching English-language learners with learning difficulties: Guiding principles and examples from research-based practice.* Reston, VA: Council for Exceptional Children.

Gottlieb, M.H. (2006). *Assessing English language learners: Bridges from language proficiency to academic achievement.* Thousand Oaks, CA: Corwin.

Grabe, W. (1991). Current developments in second language reading research. *TESOL Quarterly, 25*(3), 375–406. doi:10.2307/3586977

Gudykunst, W.B., & Kim, Y.Y. (1997). *Communicating with strangers: An approach to intercultural communication* (3rd ed.). New York: McGraw Hill.

Hahn, M.L. (2002). *Reconsidering read-aloud.* Portland, ME: Stenhouse.

Hickman, P., & Dray, B.J. (2007, March). *Differentiating language and literacy instruction and assessment for bilingual primary students with diverse learning needs.* Paper presented at the annual conference of New York State Association for Bilingual Education, Melville, NY.

Hickman, P., Pollard-Durodola, S., & Vaughn, S. (2004). Storybook reading: Improving vocabulary and comprehension for English-language learners. *The Reading Teacher, 57*(8), 720–730.

Hirsch, E.D. (2006). Building knowledge: The case for bringing content into the language arts block and for a knowledge-rich curriculum core for all children. *American Educator, 30*(1), 8–17.

Hobsbaum, A., Peters, S., Sylva, K. (1996). Scaffolding in Reading Recovery. *Oxford Review of Education, 22*(1), 17–35.

Hogan, K., & Pressley, M. (Eds.). (1997). *Scaffolding student learning: Instructional approaches and issues.* Cambridge, MA: Brookline.

Jiménez, R.T., Gersten, R., & Rivera, A. (1996). Conversations with a Chicana teacher: Supporting students' transition from native to English language instruction. *The Elementary School Journal, 96*(3), 333–341. doi:10.1086/461831

Jung, E.H. (2003). The role of discourse signaling cues in second language listening comprehension. *Modern Language Journal, 87*(4), 562–577. doi:10.1111/1540-4781.00208

Kame'enui, E.J., Carnine, D.W., Dixon, R.C., Simmons, D.C., & Coyne, M.D. (2002). *Effective teaching strategies that accommodate diverse learners* (2nd ed.). Upper Saddle River, NJ: Merrill Prentice Hall.

Kindler, A.L, (2002). *Survey of the states' limited English proficient students and available educational programs and services, 2000–2001 summary report.* Washington, DC: National Clearinghouse for English Language Acquisition and Language Instruction Educational Programs.

Krashen, S.D. (1985). *Inquiries and insights: Selected essays on second language teaching, immersion and bilingual education, and literacy.* Englewood Cliffs, NJ: Alemany.

Krashen, S.D. (1989). *Language acquisition and language education: Extension and applications.* New York: Prentice Hall.

Krashen, S.D., & Terrell, T.D. (1983). *The natural approach: Language acquisition in the classroom.* New York: Pergamon.

Lapp, D., Flood, J., Brock, C., & Fisher, D. (2007). *Teaching reading to every child.* Mahwah, NJ: Erlbaum.

Linan-Thompson, S., Vaughn, S., Hickman, P., & Kouzekanani, K. (2003). Effectiveness of supplemental reading instruction for second-grade English language learners with reading difficulties. *The Elementary School Journal, 103*(3), 221–238. doi:10.1086/499724

Lou, Y., Spence, J.C., Pulsen, C., Chambers, B., & d'Apollonia, S. (1996). Within-class grouping: A meta-analysis. *Review of Educational Research, 66*(4), 423–458.

Mathes, P.G., Linan-Thompson, S., Pollard-Duradola, S.D., Hagan, E.C., & Vaughn, S. (2003). *Lectura proactive para principantes: Intensive small group instruction for Spanish speaking readers.* Grant award by the National Institute of Child Health and Human Development (HD-99-012), Development of English Literacy in Spanish-Speaking Children.

Mathes, P.G., Torgesen, J.K., Wahl, M., Menchetti, J.C., & Grek, M.L. (1999). *Proactive beginning reading: Intensive small group instruction for struggling readers.* Grant award by the National Institute of Child Health and Human Development (#R01 HD), Prevention and Remediation of Reading Disabilities.

McLaughlin, B. (1987). Reading in a second language: Studies with adult and child learners. In S.R. Goldman & H.T. Trueba (Eds.), *Becoming literate in English as a second language* (pp. 57–70). Norwood, NJ: Ablex.

Meacham, S.J. (2001). Vygotsky and the blues: Re-reading cultural connections and conceptual development. *Theory Into Practice, 40*(3), 190–197. doi:10.1207/s15430421tip4003_7

Meacham, S.J. (2003). Headwoman's blues: Small-group reading and the interactions of culture, gender, and ability. In A.I. Willis, G.E. Garcia, R. Barrera, & V.J. Harris (Eds.), *Multicultural issues in literacy research and practice* (pp. 49–68). Mahwah, NJ: Erlbaum.

Minskoff, E.H. (2005). *Teaching reading to struggling learners*. Baltimore: Paul H. Brookes.

Moll, L.C., & González, N. (2004). Engaging life: A funds-of-knowledge approach to multicultural education. In J.A. Banks and C.A. McGee Banks (Eds.), *Handbook of research on multicultural education* (pp. 699–715). San Francisco: Jossey-Bass.

Morrow, L.M. (1987). The effect of small-group story reading on children's questions and comments. In S. McCormick & J. Zutell (Eds.), *Cognitive and social perspectives for literacy research and instruction* (37th yearbook of the National Reading Conference, pp. 77–86). Chicago: National Reading Conference.

Morrow, L.M. (1988). Young children's responses to one-to-one story readings in school settings. *Reading Research Quarterly, 23*(1), 89–107. doi:10.2307/747906

Morrow, L.M., & Brittain, R. (2003). The nature of storybook reading in the elementary school: Current practices. In A. van Kleek, S.A. Stahl, & E.B. Bauer (Eds.), *On reading books to children: Parents and teachers* (pp. 140–158). Mahwah, NJ: Erlbaum.

Morrow, L.M., & Smith, J.K. (1990). The effects of group size on interactive storybook reading. *Reading Research Quarterly, 25*(3), 213–231. doi:10.2307/748003

Moss, B. (2004). Teaching expository text structures through information trade book retellings. *The Reading Teacher, 57*(8), 710–718.

Nagy, W.E. (1988). *Teaching vocabulary to improve reading comprehension*. Newark, DE: International Reading Association.

Nagy, W.E., García, G.E., Durgunoglu, A.Y., & Hancin-Bhatt, B. (1993). Spanish-English bilingual students' use of cognates in English reading. *Journal of Reading Behavior, 25*(3), 241–259.

Nation, I.S.P. (1990). *Teaching and learning vocabulary*. Boston, MA: Heinle & Heinle.

National Clearinghouse for English Language Acquisition. (2004). *The growing numbers of limited English proficient students: 2002–2003*. Retrieved January 14, 2005, from www.ncela.gwu.edu

National Institute of Child Health and Human Development. (2000). *Report of the National Reading Panel. Teaching children to read: An evidence-based assessment of the scientific research literature on reading and its implications for reading instruction* (NIH Publication No. 00-4769). Washington, DC: U.S. Government Printing Office.

Neuman, S.B. (2006). The knowledge gap: Implications for early education. In D.K. Dickinson & S.B. Neuman (Eds.), *Handbook of early literacy research* (Vol. 2, pp. 29–40). New York: Guilford Press.

Newman, D., Griffin, P., & Cole, M. (1989). *The construction zone: Working for cognitive change in school*. New York: Cambridge University Press.

O'Malley, J.M., & Chamot, A.U. (1990). *Learning strategies in second language acquisition*. New York: Cambridge University Press.

O'Malley, J.M., Chamot, A.U., & Kupper, L. (1989). Listening comprehension strategies in second language acquisition. *Applied Linguistics, 10*(4), 438–446. doi:10.1093/applin/10.4.438

Pinnell, G.S., & Jaggar, A.M. (1991). Oral language: Speaking and listening in the classroom. In J. Flood, J.M. Jensen, D. Lapp, & J.R. Squire (Eds.), *Handbook of research on the teaching of the English language arts* (pp. 691–742). New York: Macmillan.

Ramsey, P. (1987). *Teaching and learning in a diverse world: Multicultural education for young children*. New York: Teachers College Press.

Reese, L., Garnier, H., Gallimore, R., & Goldenberg, C. (2000). Longitudinal analysis of the antecedents of emergent Spanish literacy and middle-school English reading achievement of Spanish-speaking students. *American Educational Research Journal, 37*(3), 633–662.

Roe, B.D., & Ross, E.P. (2006). *Integrating language arts through literature and thematic units*. New York: Pearson.

Rosenblatt, L.M. (1991). Literature-S.O.S.! *Language Arts, 68*(6), 444–448.

Royer, J.M., & Carlo, M.S. (1991). Transfer of comprehension skills from native to second language. *Journal of Reading, 34*(6), 450–455.

Santamaría, L.J., Fletcher, T.V., & Bos, C.S. (2002). Effective pedagogy for English language learners in inclusive classrooms. In A.J. Artiles & A.A. Ortiz (Eds.), *English language learners with special education needs: Identification, assessment, and instruction* (pp. 133–158). Washington, DC: Center for Applied Linguistics.

Scarcella, R. (2003). *Academic English: A conceptual framework* (Technical Report 2003-1). Irvine, CA: University of California Linguistic Minority Research Institute. Retrieved March 18, 2005, from lmri.ucsb.edu/publications/techreports.php

Smolkin, L.B., & Donovan, C.A. (2000). *The contexts of comprehension: Information book read alouds and comprehensive acquisition* (No. 2-009). Ann Arbor, MI: Center for the Improvement of Early Reading Achievement.

Snow, C. (2008). Cross-cutting themes and future directions. In D. August & T. Shanahan (Eds.), *Developing reading and writing in second-language learners* (pp. 275–300). New York: Routledge.

Snow, C.E., Burns, M.S., & Griffin, P. (Eds.). (1998). *Preventing reading difficulties in young children*. Washington, DC: National Academy Press.

Southern California Comprehensive Assistance Center. (1998, May). Material presented at the meeting of the Comprehensive Centers Reading Success Network, San Antonio, TX.

Stahl, S.A., & Stahl, K.A.D. (2004). Word wizards all! Teaching word meanings in preschool and primary education. In J.F. Baumann & E.J. Kame'enui (Eds.), *Vocabulary instruction: Research to practice* (pp. 59–78). New York: Guilford.

Tabors, P.O. (1997). *One child, two languages: A guide for preschool educators of children learning English as a second language*. Baltimore: Paul H. Brookes.

Teale, W.H. (2003). Reading aloud to young children as a classroom instructional activity: Insights from research and practice. In A. van Kleek, S.A. Stahl, & E.B. Bauer (Eds.), *On reading books to children* (pp. 114–139). Mahwah, NJ: Erlbaum.

Thompkins, G.E. (2005). *Language arts: Patterns of practice*. Upper Saddle River, NJ: Pearson.

Vacca, J.L., Vacca, R.T., Gove, M.K., Burkey, L., Lenhard, L.A., & McKean, C. (2003). *Reading and learning to read* (5th ed.). Boston: Allyn & Bacon.

Vacca, R.T., & Vacca, J.L. (2008). *Content area reading: Literacy and learning across the curriculum* (9th ed.). Boston: Allyn & Bacon.

Vaughn, S., Cirino, P.T., Linan-Thompson, S., Mathes, P.G., Carlson, C.D., Hagan, E.C., et al. (2006). Effectiveness of a Spanish intervention and an English intervention for English-language learners at risk for reading problems. *American Educational Research Journal, 43*(3), 449–487. doi:10.3102/00028312043003449

Vaughn, S., & Linan-Thompson, S. (2003). Group size and time allotted to intervention: Effects for students with reading difficulties. In B.R. Foorman (Ed.), *Preventing and remediating reading difficulties: Bringing science to scale* (pp. 299–324). Baltimore: York.

Vaughn, S., Linan-Thompson, S., & Hickman, P. (2003). Response to instruction as a means of identifying students with reading/learning disabilities. *Exceptional Children, 69*(4), 391–409.

Vaughn, S., Linan-Thompson, S., Mathes, P., Cárdenas-Hagan, E., Pollard-Durodola, S.D., & Francis, D. (2005). Interventions for first-grade English language learners with reading difficulties. *Perspectives, 31*(1), 31–35.

Vaughn, S., Linan-Thompson, S., Mathes, P.G., Cirino, P.T., Carlson, C.D., Pollard-Durodola, S.D., et al. (2006). Effectiveness of a Spanish intervention for first-grade English language learners at risk for reading difficulties. *Journal of Learning Disabilities, 39*(1), 56–73. doi:10.1177/00222194060390010601

Vaughn, S., Mathes, P., Linan-Thompson, S., Cirino, P., Carlson, C., Pollard-Durodola, S., et al. (2006). Effectiveness of an English intervention for first-grade English language learners at risk for reading problems. *The Elementary School Journal, 107*(2), 153–180. doi:10.1086/510653

Vaughn, S., Mathes, P.G., Linan-Thompson, S., & Francis, D.J. (2005). Teaching English-language learners at risk for reading disabilities to read: Putting research into practice. *Learning Disabilities Research & Practice, 20*(1), 58–67.

Vaughn-Shavuo, F. (1990). Using story grammar and language experience for improving recall and comprehension in the teaching of ESL to Spanish-dominant first-graders. Unpublished doctoral dissertation, Hofstra, NY.

Verhallen, M., & Schoonen, R. (1993). Lexical knowledge of monolingual and bilingual children. *Applied Linguistics, 14*(4), 344–363. doi:10.1093/applin/14.4.344

Vygotsky, L.S. (1978). *Mind in society: The development of higher psychological processes* (M. Cole, V. John-Steiner, S. Scribner, & E. Souberman, Eds. & Trans.). Cambridge, MA: Harvard University Press.

Wasik, B.A., & Bond, M.A. (2001). Beyond the pages of a book: Interactive book reading and language development in preschool classrooms. *Journal of Educational Psychology, 93*(2), 243–250. doi:10.1037/0022-0663.93.2.243

Wasik, B.A., Bond, M.A., & Hindman, A. (2005). Educating at-risk students from preschool through high school. *Yearbook of the National Society for the Study of Education, 101*(2), 89–110.

Woodcock, R.W. (1991). *Woodcock language proficiency battery-revised, English and Spanish forms: Examiner's manual.* Itasca, IL: Riverside.

Literature Cited

Bogart, J.E., & Daigneault, S. (1991). *Sara vio un guacamaya azúl*. New York: Scholastic.

Burns, M. (1997). *Spaghetti and meatballs for all: A mathematical story*. New York: Scholastic.

Carle, E. (1991) *A house for hermit crab*. New York: Scholastic.

Cherry, L. (2000). *The great kapok tree: A tale of the Amazon rain forest*. New York: Voyager.

Dorros, A. (1998). *Ant cities*. New York: HarperTrophy.

Gibbons, G. (1994). *Spiders*. New York: Holiday House.

Gibbons, G. (1996). *Cats*. New York: Holiday House.

Gibbons, G. (1997). *Dogs*. New York: Holiday House.

Gibbons, G. (2000). *The honeymakers*. New York: HarperTrophy.

Henkes, K. (1995). *Julius, the baby of the world*. New York: HarperTrophy.

Henkes, K. (1996). *Chrysanthemum*. New York: HarperCollins.

Henkes, K., & Mlawer, T. (1998). *Julio, el rey de la casa*. New York: Everest.

Hutchins, P. (1989). *The doorbell rang*. New York: HarperTrophy.

Palmer, S. (1991). *Nutrias de mar*. Vero Beach, FL: Rourke Enterprises.

Pinczes, E.J. (1997). *One hundred hungry ants*. New York: Scholastic.

Polacco, P. (1990). *Thunder Cake*. New York: Philomel.

Polacco, P. (1997). *Chicken Sunday*. New York: Philomel.

Rey, H.A. (1947). *Curious George takes a job*. New York: Houghton Mifflin.

Selsam, M.E., & Jonson, N. (1992). *Como crecen los gatitos*. New York: Scholastic.

Stone, L.M. (2001). *Las serpientes y nosotros*. Vero Beach, FL: Rourke Enterprises.

Williams, V.B. (1984). *A chair for my mother*. New York: HarperTrophy.

Williams, V.B. (1994). *Un sillón para mi mamá*. New York: Rayo.

INDEX

Note. Page numbers followed by *f* and *t* indicate figures and tables, respectively.

Hirsch, E.D., 27, 30
Hobsbaum, A., 2
Hogan, K., 19
Homogeneous grouping of students, 22–23
A House for Hermit Crab (Carle), 48, 49*t*
Hutchins, Pat, 26

I

Incidental exposure to vocabulary, 37
Inferential comprehension questions, 64–65
Inferential thinking, 4
Informational texts: exposure to, 26; listening comprehension questions from, 66*t*, 67*t*, 68*t*; structure of, 28
Instruction, in intervention program, x, 89. *See also* explicit instruction; explicit instruction; vocabulary instruction
Instructional design principles, 71, 72*t*, 73
Instructional scaffolding. *See* scaffolding
Integrating new vocabulary into conversations and activities, 55–56
Intermediate fluency stage of language development, 9*f*
Interpersonal language proficiency, 11–13, 12*t*
Intervention studies: outcomes, x–xi, 90–91; overview, x, 87–88; strategic read-aloud component, 89; teachers and curriculum, 89

J

Jaggar, A.M., 60
Janisch, C., 10
Jiménez, R.T., 19
Johnson, N., 68
Julio, el rey de la casa (Henkes & Mlawer), 71, 75
Julius, the Baby of the World (Henkes), 25, 71, 75
Jung, E.H., 62

K

Kame'enui, E.J., 19, 89
Kim, Y.Y., 3
Kindler, A.L., ix, xi
Knowledge, conceptual, drawing on and building, 30–31, 83–84
Kouzekanani, K., 18
Krashen, S.D., 7, 8, 10
Kupper, L., 58

L

Language development and listening comprehension, 68–69
Language proficiency: answering questions and, 65–66, 68; assessing, 6–7; comprehension and, 57; developing, 7–8, 9*f*; interpersonal vs. academic, 11–13, 12*t*
Lapp, D., 28
Learning: acquisition compared to, 10–11; bridging experience and, 4, 17–18, 31–33, 60–61; enculturation and, 3; moving from familiar to unknown, 3–4; sociocultural theory of, 2
Lessons: critical elements in, 71, 73; in English, 75–79, 79*t*; in intervention program, x, 89; scope and sequence, 13, 14*f*, 15, 73, 74*t*, 75; in Spanish, xi, 79–83, 83*t*
Levels: of linguistic complexity, 28–30; of text structure, 27–28; of word difficulty, 40–44, 42*t*
Linan-Thompson, S., 4, 18, 20, 22, 87, 88, 89, 90, 91
Linguistic complexity of texts, 28–30
Listening comprehension: adapting procedures, 69–70; balancing content instruction and language development, 68–69; overview of, 57–58; prereading activities, 60–61; questions,

developing and asking, 62–66, 66*t*, 67*t*, 68, 68*t*; reading aloud, approaches to, 61–62; teaching, 59–60, 61*t*; types of, 58–59, 59*t*

LISTENING FOR WORDS IN TEXTS, 52–53, 54*f*, 55–56

LITERACY, FIRST-LANGUAGE, 4–6

LITERAL COMPREHENSION QUESTIONS, 64–65

LOU, Y., 22

M

MARKS, S.U., 10

MATERIALS SCAFFOLDING, 20, 21*t*

MATHES, P.G., x, 4, 22, 87, 88, 89, 90, 91

MAXIMIZING COMPREHENSIBLE INPUT, 10

MCKEOWN, M.G., 39

MCLAUGHLIN, B., 91

MEACHAM, S.J., 3, 20, 22

MEANING FOR WORD, CREATING, 45–46, 48*t*

MENCHETTI, J.C., 89

MINSKOFF, E.H., 47, 50

MLAWER, T., 71, 75

MODELING OF SKILLS, 2

MOLL, L.C., 3

MONTES, J.A., 10

MORROW, L.M., ix, 4, 20, 22, 37, 50, 55, 61, 62

MOSS, B., 26

N

NAGY, W.E., 3, 40

NARRATIVE TEXTS: listening comprehension questions from, 66*t*, 67*t*; structure of, 27–28; vocabulary development and, 35

NATION, I.S.P., 56

NATIONAL CLEARINGHOUSE FOR ENGLISH LANGUAGE ACQUISITION, ix

NATIONAL INSTITUTE OF CHILD HEALTH AND HUMAN DEVELOPMENT (NICHD), 35, 36, 37, 38, 39, 53, 60, 69, 91

NATIVE-LANGUAGE LITERACY, 4–6

NEUMAN, S.B., 84

NEWMAN, D., 3

NONFICTION TEXTS. *See* informational texts

NUTRIAS DE MAR (PALMER), 51*t*

O

O'MALLEY, J.M., 8, 11, 18, 19, 58

ONE HUNDRED HUNGRY ANTS (PINCZES), 26

ORAL LANGUAGE SKILLS, BUILDING, 65–66, 68, 84

ORGANIZATIONAL PATTERNS OF TEXT STRUCTURE, 27–28

OUTCOMES OF INTERVENTION PROGRAM, x–xi, 90–91

P

PALMER, S., 51*t*

PARALLELS, DRAWING, 32

PERFORMANCE-ORIENTED APPROACH, 61–62

PETERS, S., 2

PINCZES, ELINOR J., 26

PINNELL, G.S., 60

PLANNING VOCABULARY PORTION OF LESSONS, 37–38, 38*f*

POLACCO, PATRICIA, 25, 44